WHAT OTHERS ARE SAYING

THE RECTOR, THE VESTRY, AND THE BISHOP (2023)

In Anglicanism, the relationship, distinct roles, and common vision between the vestry, the rector, and the bishop are crucial. Roseberry has created a thoughtful and practical guide for church leaders as they serve the Lord and God's people. Understanding what he has shared will not only limit potential conflict but will empower strong partnerships so that the Gospel mission can go forth in clarity and purpose.

— THE MOST REV. DR. FOLEY BEACH,
ARCHBISHOP AND PRIMATE OF THE
ANGLICAN CHURCH IN NORTH AMERICA

Canon Roseberry took an already substantial book and made it even better with additional material. The imagery and explanations about the way the bishop relates with Parish leadership are extremely helpful. Anyone entering into leadership in the Anglican Church or desiring a refresher on vestry service would benefit greatly from this fine new edition!

— THE RIGHT REV. DR. BILL ATWOOD, DEAN FOR INTERNATIONAL AFFAIRS AND BISHOP OF THE INTERNATIONAL DIOCESE, ANGLICAN CHURCH IN NORTH AMERICA

Having planted a new church in the past year, the insights written in this book are enabling our small but growing congregation, and especially our leadership, to be formed and nurtured in the beauty and best of our Anglican tradition.

— THE VENERABLE MICHAEL J. MCKINNON, CHURCH OF THE ADVENT, SOUTHERN PINES, NC

As a former rector, David Roseberry's book, *The Rector, the Vestry, and the Bishop,* offers invaluable guidance for leading a congregation within the Anglican tradition. Though the scriptures and Christ's teachings in the Gospels show Christians the path, few resources address the practicalities of shepherding God's flock day-to-day within an Anglican context. Based on his experience and coaching, Roseberry provides an essential roadmap, delineating the roles and relationships between the rector, vestry, and bishop. Any ordained leader hoping to nurture their congregation while cooperating with church leadership effectively will find this book a trove of insights and practical wisdom. This is essential reading for anyone seeking to walk in Christ's footsteps while guiding others.

— THE REV. DR. JED ROSEBERRY, RECTOR,
RESTORATION ANGLICAN CHURCH,
RICHARDSON, TX

The first edition of this book has been an enormous help to me in my work with two different vestries, and this new edition will prove to be even more valuable. There are many vestry members and rectors who don't really understand their unique roles in Anglican polity, and this book helps to fill in the gaps. David brings his practical wisdom from his years of experience and presents it in a way that is applicable to all sizes of Anglican congregations. I would highly recommend buying a copy for every member of your vestry!

— THE REV. CHRISTOPHER M. KLUKAS,
RECTOR, ST. ANDREW'S ANGLICAN
CHURCH, LEWIS CENTER, OH

In *The Rector, the Vestry, and the Bishop*, David Roseberry provides church leaders with a thoughtful and practical guide for understanding roles within Anglican polity. This expanded new edition does a wonderful job of clearly explaining the bishop's role and relationship to parish leadership. I highly recommend this book as an essential resource for vestries, rectors, and bishops who want to work together effectively for God's mission.

— THE RIGHT REV. KEITH ANDREWS,
BISHOP, DIOCESE OF WESTERN
ANGLICANS, ANGLICAN CHURCH IN
NORTH AMERICA

THE RECTOR AND THE VESTRY (PREVIOUS EDITION, 2020)

This book is now required reading for all new members of the Vestry at Apostles-by-the-Sea. And I know I'll be referring to it often in the years ahead as our Church continues to grow!

— THE REV. JOHN WALLACE, RECTOR,
APOSTLES-BY-THE-SEA, SANTA ROSA
BEACH, FL

I wish I had this book when I first joined our Vestry, I would have been more prepared. Rev. Canon David Roseberry gives excellent advice on the roles of the Vestry and of the Rector. In his introduction he says he wrote this book to "assist and empower every vestry and rector to be unified, effective, and focused," and I believe he accomplished that with this book. His chapters on financial concerns and best practices are very helpful. It should be a "must read" book for anyone wanting to serve on a Vestry!

— MIKE AND AMBER W.

A wealth of information for Rectors as well as new Vestry members.

— MEGHAN WILSON

Well done! Canon Roseberry's choice of using creative metaphors and anecdotes while avoiding institutional jargon made the culture, concepts, and practice of our ACNA parish ministry very accessible and applicable. For our day, with so many new to Anglicanism and parochial leadership, his book is far more useful than the Alban Institute material I have taught with over the years. I will be seeing that every congregation leader in our diocese receives a copy (and budget the same for the wardens in the coming year).

— THE RIGHT REV. KEVIN ALLEN, BISHOP
OF CASCADIA, ANGLICAN CHURCH IN
NORTH AMERICA

Loved the clarity and practicality of this book. Canon Roseberry draws on the best of other manuals and offers his own helpful advice. The chapters on the role of the rector and the wardens are absolute gold and a must for onboarding new vestry members.

— THE REV. NATHAN HALE

I especially appreciate the historical perspective of Anglican polity. I am fairly new to Anglicanism, and *The Rector and the Vestry* provided great information related to the role and function of the vestry.

— DODE WORSHAM

I helped start an Anglican church seven years ago and, boy, would this book have been helpful! Canon Roseberry has provided much-needed help for vestries that are learning how to lead an Anglican church well. Even though our parish has learned a lot through trial and error, we're using *The Rector and the Vestry* to rethink our vestry role description and best practices as a governing board. Thanks, Canon Roseberry!

— THE REV. ROB PATTERSON

To Jed.

I am so proud to see the faithful man,

husband, son, and pastor you have become.

Anglican Compass, Inc.

Copyright © 2020, 2023 (revised, 2nd edition) by David H. Roseberry

ISBN: 9798871276051

ANGLICAN COMPASS, INC.
3001 VEROT SCHOOL RD.
LAFAYETTE, LA 70508
WWW.ANGLICANCOMPASS.COM

PUBLISHED IN THE UNITED STATES OF AMERICA

THE RECTOR, THE VESTRY, AND THE BISHOP

The Essential Guide for Anglican Leaders

DAVID H. ROSEBERRY

ANGLICAN COMPASS

CONTENTS

FOREWORD

THE MOST REV. ROBERT DUNCAN, D.D.

I am delighted to write a foreword for the new edition of this book. The first release, *The Rector and the Vestry*, was an invaluable resource for the vestries and rectors of congregations in the Anglican Church in North America (ACNA). I have used it extensively in my own ministry to parish leadership. As a former diocesan bishop and first archbishop, I recognized the need for precisely this kind of comprehensive guide that explains our polity and practices, enabling our churches to prosper and grow.

David Roseberry, a dear friend and brother in Christ whom I have known for over two decades, has done a remarkable job improving this second edition, *The Rector, the Vestry, and the Bishop*. He rightly emphasizes the importance of honoring and strengthening the relationships between the rector, the vestry, and the bishop of the diocese.

I am particularly pleased that Canon Roseberry consulted with numerous bishops, including myself, to write the chapters on the purpose of a bishop and their role within a diocese and its congregations. His clear articulation of the significance of this office, along with his summary statements, is particularly helpful as we seek to be Anglicans together at our best.

David Roseberry's extensive experience and deep personal commitment to the growth and flourishing of our churches make him an ideal author for this book. His unparalleled work in founding and developing Christ Church (Plano), one of the largest congregations in our Province, has provided him with invaluable insights. Having led numerous vestry meetings throughout his thirty-year tenure, David understands the rector's pivotal role in a congregation's life. The experiences and training he has acquired have shaped the content of this book, making it a rich source of wisdom and guidance.

Also, acknowledging the remarkable contributions to our Province made by Canon David is right in this context. He has consistently stepped forward, often before anyone recognized the need, to address critical issues. Initiatives such as hosting the influential conference "A Place to Stand," hosting my consecration and investiture as the first Archbishop, serving as Board Chairman of Trinity School for Ministry, establishing the church planting movement Anglican 1000, and founding Matthew25 to serve those in need reflect his unwavering dedication to the Anglican Church in North America.

I firmly believe that the extensive research, writing, and development of *The Rector, the Vestry, and the Bishop* is yet another way in which David has provided our Province with what we truly need. I wholeheartedly recommend this book to every rector, vestry member, and bishop within our Province. May rectors utilize it to teach and train their vestries, vestries employ it to support and enhance the vision and leadership of their rectors, and bishops incorporate it as they lead their dioceses in strengthening the indispensable ministry of our rectors, vestries, and congregations.

David Roseberry has my utmost appreciation for his diligent research, exceptional writing, and unwavering commitment to developing this valuable resource. On behalf of all who will benefit from this book, both now and in the future, I express our deepest gratitude.

The Most Rev. Robert Duncan, D.D.
Archbishop of the Anglican Church in North America, 2009–2014
Seventh Bishop of Pittsburgh
Trinitytide, 2023

INTRODUCTION
WITH A PREFACE TO THE 2ND EDITION

THREE THINGS ALL ANGLICAN CHURCHES HAVE IN COMMON

I have had the privilege of working with churches and their diverse leaders who are all dedicated to serving God and advancing His kingdom. In recent years, I have met passionate, kingdom-minded individuals who tirelessly commit to their church's mission. These leaders are intelligent, eager, and devoted to their congregations, whether new or experienced.

These leaders come from various backgrounds and perspectives. Some are new to Anglicanism, while others are former Episcopalians or members of other established traditions. Some are just discovering the beauty and forms of Anglicanism and participating in new congregations.

And the churches they lead are often as diverse in liturgical styles and traditions as their leaders. A person looking for a home church needs only to pull up the "church finder" map on the ACNA website and look around. In some areas of the country, there are many congregations to explore. But each of them is diverse and unique. Not all Anglican congregations are the same, to be sure.

Despite their diversity, these congregations share three critical elements in common. First, each church has a rector, an elected and appointed leader committed to serving the congregation. Second, each church has a group of laypeople elected or selected by a vote to support and lead the congregation. This group is named differently depending on the congregation. Most commonly, this group is called a vestry. Finally, each church has a bishop responsible for the life and health of the congregation in the context of a larger diocesan family.

AN ANGLICAN TROIKA

It would be a surprise to find a Russian word in a book on Anglican polity, but it fits beautifully. A *troika* is a team of three horses, for example, who are tied together and who work together to pull something forward. Indeed, it is so with these three: the rector, the vestry, and the bishop are united by their love for Jesus Christ and commitment to proclaiming the Gospel and effectively administering the church's sacraments. And they must work together to accomplish their united task.

The *rector* is the chief visionary leader for the congregation. The *vestry* plays a vital role in leading and developing the congregation. The *bishop* superintends the congregation and networks it into the rest of the congregations in the diocese. Those three functions are born by people who are all committed to the Gospel of Jesus Christ and its broad impact in the community and around the world.

Despite different styles of worship, sizes, contexts, emphases, practices, and programs, all Anglican congregations are similar in this way: they each have a rector leading, a governing vestry governing, and an overseeing bishop[1].

THE CHALLENGE FACING EVERY ANGLICAN CHURCH

Despite these commonalities, a clear understanding of the roles of each of these is not common. This is challenging for those who are new to the Anglican Church or are considering serving on a vestry.

To complicate matters further, many of our clergy and parishioners in the ACNA come from other church backgrounds or no Christian background. This means that they may bring to the table experiences from non-profit boards and other church governing bodies that are not aligned with Anglican polity. Some of the bishops in the College of Bishops are new to Anglicanism as well. They may not be steeped in Anglican polity, or they bring a wealth of experience from other traditions that may not easily apply.

Consider a sample vestry from churches in the Anglican Church in North America. Here is a random list of people who might be serving as members of your vestry:

- Bill is a seasoned Christian who joined the church after leading an elder board in his previous Bible church. He has a deep understanding of church governance and is a valuable addition to the team. He is eager to apply biblical principles to the structure of the congregation.
- Mary, Phil, and Frank bring their wealth of knowledge from their Methodist backgrounds to the congregation. They are experts on committees and understand the importance of reporting back to the board. They are expecting to serve on committees of the vestry.
- Tom's wife nominated him for the vestry, and it was a wise decision. Although he has no prior experience on a

church board, Tom is the respected chairman of a local nonprofit. His leadership and public presentation skills could be useful.

- Marcie is a passionate new Christian who is eager to serve the Lord in any way. She is an active volunteer in the youth program and wants to ensure the youth are well-represented at vestry meetings. She wants to see young people engaged at every level of the church's life.

- Kevin is a Nigerian-born immigrant who has been an integral part of the Anglican Church outside of Lagos, Nigeria. He also attended an Anglican parish in England during his graduate studies. Kevin's friendly demeanor has made him a beloved usher in our church. He can hardly wait to meet the bishop.

- Fr. Steve is the young and energetic rector who was called to bring a fresh perspective to the parish. With a background in Young Life from a large Presbyterian congregation, he is passionate about youth ministry. He wants to use the high-energy velocity of the Young Life meeting to bring new life to the congregation.

The future of this congregation is exciting, but I'm sure you can see the challenge that awaits a vestry as diverse as this. There are multiple types of experiences, backgrounds, expectations, and hopes for this elected body. If efforts in evangelism, outreach, and church planting across the Anglican Church in North America are successful, this kind of vestry will be more and more prevalent in the years to come.

This book is written to help rectors, vestry members, and bishops understand their roles and the roles of the two other counterparts. It is written to help and empower each vestry, rector, and bishop to become as unified, effective, and focused as possible.

WHO SHOULD READ THIS BOOK?

This book is written for several audiences:

- It is written for the rector and vestry of a church to distribute among their current vestry and nominees to speed up the orientation process. Often it will take months, if not close to a year, for elected vestry members to "get the hang of it." After three decades of forming and leading vestries, I often heard from the outgoing class, "I am so glad that I served on this vestry. I have seen God move in our church...and in me!"

- It is written for so-called "Rookie Anglicans" who have been nominated to serve or who want to know how their local parish works. One of the great things happening in our denomination is the influx of those who have discovered the Anglican Way in their adult years. This is even true of our ordained leaders. Anglican polity (a term we will define shortly) has clear implications for every church, and those new to the Anglican Way will significantly benefit from a book like this.

- It is written for the rector of the congregation, who is looking for something to use to develop a stronger team of leaders on the vestry. The rector of your congregation is my hero. I love the work that rectors do, and for many years, I have shared in their burden-bearing. I wrote this book for them. Rectors are the final "gatekeepers" for how the vestry operates, subject to the leadership of the bishop. But I hope the rector of your congregation will be empowered and strengthened to attempt greater things for God and do them!

- It is also written for the bishops of the Anglican Church in North America. They are godly men who are forging ahead to build our new province. Most of them were rectors at one time; some still are. They have led their fair share of vestry meetings in their parishes. Since the bishop's role is to develop a culture of governance and strength for the churches under his pastoral care, I hope this book will be useful in that process.

WHY A SECOND EDITION?

When I published the first edition, called *The Rector and the Vestry*, in early 2020, I knew some subjects required more attention. Some topics were relegated to the Appendix with a brief mention. But over the last few years, I saw gaps in the book that needed to be addressed. There were a few concepts that warranted a fuller treatment. And, of course, COVID changed a lot of things, including what should be in a book like this.

This book is an expanded Second Edition. It builds on elements in the First Edition. But in many ways, it is an entirely new book. It is nearly 25% longer!

I added chapters about the office and role of the bishop, which I think is a critical enhancement. I unpacked the model for organizing ministry that I used as a rector for over three decades: the **WEDCAP** model. I expanded an explanation of the rector's role in vision-casting and the vestry's role in succession planning. I added a few other features, which are in the **Appendix**.

In addition, I combed the original text to eliminate wordiness, enhance readability, and correct any confusing passages. My aim is to optimize this resource's usefulness for its niche, yet surprisingly broad, audience.

My hope is that these additions will serve our church and our leaders more effectively. Our tribe in the Anglican Church in

North America, though small, is made mighty through our reliance on God's strength. May this updated resource play a small role in fostering our health and clarifying our vision.

Soli Deo Gloria!

The Rev. Canon David H. Roseberry

> *Glory to God, whose power working in us can do infinitely more than we can ask or imagine. Glory to him, from generation to generation, in the church and in Christ Jesus. Amen!*

— EPHESIANS 3:20-21

---

1. My intention is to capitalize the rector, the vestry, and the bishop when referring to a specific person or office. I will not use capitals when referring to a generic role or position. But sometimes both are possible. I assume the reader will make allowances for my choices.

CHAPTER 1

YOUR CHURCH CHANGES THE WORLD

ON A MISSION TRANSCENDING TIME AND CULTURE

The Church is the only institution that exists primarily for the benefit of those who are not its members. [1]

— WILLIAM TEMPLE, ARCHBISHOP OF CANTERBURY 1942-1944

From the outside, your church may look like just another place where people regularly meet. But step inside the space *when* the people are meeting, and where the Good News of Jesus is preached and the Sacraments duly administered, and you'll find you've entered the beating heart of the most world-altering, life-changing movement in history.

YOUR AMAZING CHURCH

Do you grasp the true nature of your church? What does your community of faith signify? It might sound exaggerated, but your church is part of a broader, global network of churches. Together, they form the most enduring, significant, self-sustaining, self-renewing, mission-oriented organization on Earth. Remembering this fact is crucial.

God has a providential plan for the world and, through the influence and power of the Holy Spirit, he calls people to live under the gracious rule of the Lord Jesus Christ. Your church is a linchpin for this to happen. It is the central means through which God calls, guides, and sends people to bear witness to him and to transform individuals, families, communities, nations, and people groups one generation after another. No other organization on earth carries such a high purpose and clear mission.

As C. S. Lewis wrote:

The church exists solely to bring people to Christ, to transform them into His likeness. If it fails to do so, all the cathedrals, clergy, missions, sermons, and even the Bible itself become mere wasteful endeavors. God became human for no other reason. One could even question whether the entire universe was created for any other purpose.

— MERE CHRISTIANITY (CHAPTER 8)

THE GREAT COMMISSION AND THE CHURCH

When Jesus gave the Great Commission to his disciples after the resurrection, he did so when they were gathered together. He did not assign each of them a personal mission to explore and develop an adherence and a private understanding of the Gospel individually. Christianity is not a solo performance or an individual effort to live a Christian life either.

The Risen Christ gave the Great Commission to a collective group. He gave it to *them*, plural! A brief examination of the New Testament Scriptures confirms this fact. Although Jesus appeared to individual disciples one by one, and the Resurrection's Good News was revealed to a few here and there, he delayed the announcement of the mission until they were gathered together. When Thomas missed the initial visit of Jesus to his disciples, Jesus did not seek him out for a personal, private encounter. He waited until the disciples were (again) assembled, and then he revealed himself to Thomas and the rest of them. Together.

Even the Apostle Paul, who had the most personal and individualized encounter with Christ among anyone in the New Testament, was immediately brought to a group, an unnamed church as yet, to recover and reshape his thinking. He was escorted to a place where he could be nurtured and protected, not by secret angels and personal attendants, but by the church.

THE EARLY CHURCH ORGANIZES

The new believers were summoned to a mission. They were called to go out. But they were not to go as individuals. As we witness in the Gospel accounts, the Book of Acts, and the letters in the New Testament, the Good News of Jesus Christ reached ordinary men and women and compelled them to learn to collaborate—together—for the sake of the mission. Thanks be to God; the Holy Spirit took them and made them catalytic converters for the rest of the world!

Guided by the Holy Spirit, a fully self-sustaining organization emerged to carry the Gospel forward from one generation to the next. This is a remarkable occurrence in the New Testament narrative. Jesus called fishermen, tax collectors, sinners, and ordinary individuals to be disciples. Within a single generation, these men and women had established a robust organizational framework for this expanding group of ordinary people that would change the world. This, in itself, is a miracle!

THE CHURCH RESILIENT

As I sat down to write the first edition of this book, my wife and I had just moved into a new apartment complex in North Plano. From our 10th-story unit, we had a clear view of Plano, North Dallas, and the massive former international headquarters of Electronic Data Systems. This building rose above the North Texas prairie in its heyday, replacing acres of grasslands. Its 1.6 million square feet of offices, conference rooms, training centers, and personnel support services were a colossal feat of architectural engineering designed to dominate its industry for the next century. *Or so it was thought.*

Today, the EDS building stands empty, and its acres of structured parking are abandoned. The company is no more. This once-mighty Fortune 500 corporation made a few leadership mistakes and failed to anticipate the shift in business models that the Internet would bring. Can you imagine it? The data processing king was caught off guard.

TOO BIG TO FAIL?

They eventually retracted, downsized, and sold off all their parts and profit centers. They fell apart. And so, the monumental achievement, the massive headquarters that once loomed large in my city, now stands empty. Empty! I am sure the stockholders and corporate leaders believed EDS was too big to fail. Yet, the truth is that the businesses and organizations in which we place our trust are just passing through. They will all change, and they will eventually fade away.

The same can be said of governments. Monarchies, the oldest form of government in the world, revolve around one person's rule. Democracy, the most prevalent form of government worldwide, has a long-standing history in the United States. However, we know that monarchies end, and other forms of government either fade away or transform into different structures.

Given enough time, all things change.

However, the church is different. It has faced countless challenges throughout its history and has even been declared dead on many occasions. Yet, the church has always discovered ways to renew itself and carry on its mission. The church has traversed ages and cultures, embraced various peoples and nations, and influenced everything it has encountered. It stands as the oldest continuously renewing and reforming organization that has ever existed.

The church endures from generation to generation not because it is too big to fail, but because it is alive.

Today, when we contemplate businesses and their ability to withstand the unpredictable forces of markets, recessions, labor, supply, and demand, we are impressed by any company that surpasses 25 years of existence. A hundred-year-old company would astound us. I recently read about the world's oldest continuously operating company, a 700-year-old family-run furniture maker in Italy. Truly impressive!

However, in comparison, the church's 2000-year history is an undeniable miracle. And your congregation, as part of this enduring institution, stands at the forefront of a movement that is still changing the world. The church alters everything it touches. It is vital to remember this fact and approach the church's work with the reverence and dedication it deserves.

IN OTHER WORDS, YOUR CONGREGATION, THE FAMILY OF believers with whom you grow in faith and learn about our Lord Jesus and his outward mission, occupies the leading edge of this movement. This awareness should transform the way your church operates. A church with an eternal and evergreen mission can overcome obstacles and setbacks with incredible momentum.

Therefore, if you serve as the rector, an ordained leader, a nominated vestry candidate, or an elected/appointed member of the vestry, or an elected and consecrated bishop, please remember that your role is not limited to running the church, building programs, raising funds, or administering a diocese. While these tasks are important and must be attended to, they do not define the church's mission.

You have been ordained, called, chosen, nominated, elected or consecrated to be a faithful steward of this God-blessed, Christ-centered, Holy Spirit-empowered, faith-based, enduring, and world-changing enterprise. This is the work to which you are called.

---

1. Quote from his book, *Christianity and Social Order.*

CHAPTER 2

THE ANGLICAN THIRD WAY

A BLENDED MODEL OF CHURCH GOVERNANCE

Our vocation is to build up the body of Christ, not tear it down over secondary issues.[1]

— JOHN GUERNSEY, ANGLICAN BISHOP,
ACNA

WHAT IS ECCLESIASTICAL POLITY?

"**A**nglicanism has been described as having a 'third way' between Roman Catholicism and Protestantism, which allows for a generosity of spirit." – Urban T. Holmes, Episcopal Priest and Professor at The University of the South, *What is Anglicanism.*

Now, we can turn to some of the details about church governance and the unique way that Anglican churches are led and governed.

But to do that, I need to introduce a phrase that you may never have used, let alone heard: "Ecclesiastical Polity".

First, let's understand what the word "polity" means. It is not often used in regular street speech, but, as you can see, it has something to do with the word "politics." A wordsmith would know that the Greek word for city is "polis." Polity is related to both of these and refers to how a group of people governs themselves as a community. A "polity" is a set of rules and standards that are agreed upon by the group. If you see the word "ecclesiastical" ("ecclesia" means the "gathered ones," i.e., the church) in the first position, you have an endlessly interesting subject: Ecclesiastical Polity.[2]

Let me show you how interesting it can be.

ONLY TWO KINDS OF CHURCHES?

A few years ago, while I was leading a vestry meeting, one of our members asked to make a point about church polity. That alone impressed me. Luke was a skilled attorney in his practice but had been mostly silent in our previous sessions. He didn't say much, but people listened when he spoke. He observed, *David, I have been reading about churches and how they hold property titles and govern themselves. I have seen there are only two kinds of churches in the world: congregational and hierarchical.*

He went on to say that congregational churches are self-contained, self-governed, and mostly independent. They are organizations with their charter, by-laws, constitution, and governing boards. Some of these congregational churches can even ordain their ministers. They have their statement of beliefs or confessional statements. Churches like this may draw upon the help or resources of other churches like them. They can form associations, networks, or even missional relationships to do their mission or train leaders. There is no shortage of this kind of church, both large and small.

Then he described the other model for church governance and leadership: the hierarchical church. These churches exist as part of a structured hierarchy. They might appear self-governed, but they are subject to the supervision and direction of a hierarchy over them. A bishop, a superintendent, or some judicatory in authority "oversees" the church's work. Codes of conduct, standards, and clear boundaries of belief hold believers together as a coherent family.

The "Seven Sisters" of mainline American Protestant Christianity are typically the most hierarchical churches in the USA. They are the United Methodist Church, the Christian Church (Disciples of Christ), the Presbyterian Church, the Episcopal Church, the Evangelical Lutheran Church in America, the American Baptist Churches, and the United Church of Christ.

Roman Catholic and Orthodox congregations are also hierarchical, with Bishops, Archbishops, and other systems and leaders "above" the congregation.

NIGHT AND DAY

This was Luke's point: congregational and hierarchical churches and their forms of government are as different as night and day. They may have the same mission—to preach Christ as Lord—but they have very different modalities. The congregational model has unique blessings, features, and problems, as do the churches of the hierarchical model. But one kind of church is radically different from the other in its governance, decision-making, membership requirements, outreach efforts in their community, use of traditions and statements of faith, music selection, ordination requirements, and nearly every other component of their life.

The two types of churches can have fellowship together, but only if they are clear on the terms of their fellowship and avoid mixing or mingling their respective polities. These churches can collaborate on local mission projects, sponsor a food pantry, or even co-host an evangelistic community-wide crusade. However, these joint efforts are only temporary and cannot be sustained due to differences in governance and polity.

The elder board of a congregational church has a specific perspective on its role in the church. They are appointed for life or until they resign and are typically male with theological training and well-formed opinions. A local Bible church, for example, would not call an ordained Methodist pastor their "Senior Pastor" without a thorough recertification program, if at all.

On the other hand, the hierarchical church has a rotating body of men and women who serve on the leadership council or session. They do not necessarily have theological training but are laypeople from the pews who love their church. A Presbyterian congregation would not re-ordain a Bible Church minister without involvement and permission from the up-line hierarchy.

Bible churches may even require re-baptism for new adult members as they join the congregation. This is not due to a lack of respect for the original baptism but because baptism holds different meanings for different denominations. For Episcopalians, baptism means initiation and denominational identity, while for Bible Churches, it means conversion and congregational membership.

In summary, congregational and hierarchical churches have vastly different forms of government, and their models come with their respective problems. However, a third type of church blends both models together: the Anglican Way. This unique approach draws from the strengths of both models to create a more balanced and holistic system of church governance.

THE THIRD WAY OF ANGLICANISM

There are indeed only two kinds of churches in the world: congregational and hierarchical. But Anglicanism blends the two together to form a third type. Like many things in the Anglican tradition, there is a third way: the Anglican Way.

The Anglican Church in North America (ACNA) offers a third way, a blend of the congregational and hierarchical forms of government grounded in theological and historical reasons. The ACNA leans towards congregationalism in matters such as style, focus, mission, employment of clergy, and the incurrence and payment of debts. However, when it comes to accountability, theological beliefs, training, ordination of leaders, worship life, liturgy, and teaching, the ACNA leans towards hierarchical governance.

Do not skip over the next chapter. We are going to detail this interesting, challenging, and fascinating third way.

---

1. from a speech at the Anglican Church in North America Provincial Assembly, 2014.
2. Note: there is a glossary of titles, terms, and technicals for the Anglican Church in the Appendix.

CHAPTER 3

GOVERNING THE ANGLICAN WAY

ANGLICAN CONGREGATIONS ARE LOCALLY GUIDED YET GLOBALLY CONNECTED

The Anglican way is to seek the mind of Christ through scripture, tradition and reason.[1]

— GREG VENABLES, FORMER PRIMATE OF THE ANGLICAN CHURCH OF SOUTH AMERICA

The polity of the Anglican Church in North America is designed to offer a unique approach that recognizes the local congregation as the primary unit of mission for the Anglican Church. The congregations are responsible for making disciples of Jesus Christ on behalf of the church. However, they also secure their own property titles, raise their own budget, and make their own decisions about their program, mission, and focus. There are no denominational subsidies that keep the congregations afloat.

However, each congregation and clergy member adheres to an essential body of beliefs and practices set by the wider church and their individual bishops. The "higher authorities" in the ACNA, the bishops, exert a spiritual, moral, persuasive, and mission-defining authority over clergy and congregations. It is a non-legal authority. Indeed, the ordained leader and congregation are free to stay linked to the province and remain under their bishop and diocese—or leave if they so choose. There is a lot of freedom in this so-called "Third Way." Its success relies heavily on the relational strength of the bishop and the congregation's rector.

This blended form of governance is the ecclesiastical polity of the ACNA. We rely heavily on the local congregational leader to lead locally and the regional, diocesan leader to oversee regionally.

In summary, our ecclesiastical polity is congregational freedom to engage in mission, combined with diocesan oversight to guide and direct the effort. It is neither top-down nor bottom-up. It is inter-connected. This is the Anglican Third Way.

The role of the bishop with the congregation will be discussed later in this book. However, it is essential to note that this unique blend of congregational and hierarchical leadership works itself out in a way that is distinctive and effective for the ACNA.

UNIQUE YET CONNECTED CONGREGATIONS

The mission of the ACNA is to *Reach North America with the Transforming Love of Jesus Christ*. It is a good mission statement. But, like all mission statements, it needs to be actualized. We need to see it in action. We need to ask *how* this will get done.

Here is the plan: every church, every congregation, led by the rector and vestry, is charged to fulfill this mission. Our Constitution and Canons say that the church's primary mission is to be carried out by the local congregation. The provincial and diocesan structures serve and empower the faith community as they engage the church's mission.

But even though each of the congregations independently determines how they will fulfill the mission, *they are not independent.* Our congregational polity is also hierarchical. There is an ordered relationship between each congregation and its bishop. Collaboration and encouragement exist between congregations (rector and vestry) and their bishops. Appropriate canonical checks and balances govern these systems and relationships.

It is beyond the scope of this book to outline how a diocese governs itself and how the College of Bishops governs itself. Those topics are for another day. But this blended Anglican polity that we have highlights the serious and central role of the rector and vestry in their relationship with their bishop.

TO ILLUSTRATE: A FRANCHISE?

An analogy may serve well here. The Constitution and Canons of the ACNA state that each congregation is the clear owner of its property and all the aspects that entail. If a congregation owns a piece of land, then it holds its own title. If they have a mortgage, the congregation holds the deed of trust that secures the land. In other words, the diocese or the Province is not a part-owner of the congregation's property.

In addition, each congregation has its own unique style. They do their own marketing and train their staff, clergy, and lay leaders to work in their churches. Even if a congregation does not own property (and many do not, as they are new and young), they are still the chief determiners of what they will lease, use, rent, and perhaps, one day own.

Each Anglican congregation must exert energetic focus, strength, and commitment to become sustainable. The diocese will not take over if the mission stalls in one congregation.

In the language of business, the individual congregation is not a "franchise" unit out in the field; they are wholly "owned" by the local board of governance or the vestry. Still, at the same time, the local congregation is like a franchise unit that must be connected to the network of other churches in a diocese. Together, they should offer a common set of doctrinal and worship practices. There is room for each church to be its unique self with its own identity, practices, and emphasis. But the congregation cannot be vastly different from the rest. It must have the same tenets and tenor as the rest of the tribe, as it were.

To be crude, if a network of restaurants belongs to a brand that serves chicken, they should all serve chicken, not burgers.

Furthermore, when it comes to the mission of the ACNA to reach North America with the transforming love of Jesus Christ, each congregation is called to embody this mission as strongly and clearly as possible. But they are not to do this alone; they remain in partnered fellowship with their bishop. Each congregation is called to the good and faithful stewardship of this mission under God, but always as partners with other congregations in the same diocese.

Do you see the potential tension in this arrangement? The phrase "remain in partnered fellowship with their bishop" presents a potential area of conflict. The congregation (led by a rector) is the local branch of mission and functions independently from any hands-on oversight of the bishop. But still, the diocese (led by a bishop) is responsible for the congregation's commitment to the church's doctrine, discipline, and worship.

We will come back to this tension in the chapter on the role of the bishop and the principle of subsidiarity. But for now, note that each congregation is like a franchise striving to present the Gospel of Jesus Christ in the context of an Anglican congregation. Yet, at the same time, the bishop is responsible for the integrity and content of their ministry.

This is a very interesting dynamic that every vestry member needs to understand and appreciate. It is why every church is expected to contribute time and money to the health and vitality of its own diocese. The church is a local group with a very localized ministry that arises from the heartbeat of the congregation. Yet, at the same time, each congregation is expected to "hold fast" to the Anglican ethos of its diocese.

This is where the canons of the church come in. In a very real way, congregations are linked to their diocese and the diocese to the province through an approved set of rules, standards, written codes of conduct, and assumptions.

The term "canon" may seem unfamiliar to new vestry members. In its simplest form, a "canon" is a rule or law that can be applied to various contexts. For instance, it can refer to the established texts of the Old and New Testaments, known as "the Canon of Scripture." Alternatively, it can refer to a person working on behalf of a diocese or cathedral, as in the case of "Canon Smith." However, vestries must understand that a "canon" specifically denotes a written code of church law that makes up our "polity," or way of doing things. Although the spelling differs from that of the ballistic ordinance ("cannon"), church canons are still influential.

Church canons are organized by titles and sections codified and adopted by the governing board of a diocese or the national church. The diocese and the national body of the Anglican Church in North America maintain lists of canons.

It is worth noting that congregations do not have canons. Instead, they have by-laws and policies that should be made available to members. By-laws typically briefly describe how an individual congregation is organized and functions internally.

PROVINCIAL AND DIOCESAN CANONS

With all this said, some Canons of the Anglican Church in North America concern congregations, rectors, and, by extension, vestries. You will also want to refer to your diocese's governance documents and your congregation's by-laws for clarity and local precision.[2]

As we look at the canons of the ACNA, we can see the role and purpose of the local congregation. For example, Canon 6 of the ACNA asserts the primacy of the local congregation as the fundamental agency of the church's mission, reminding us that the chief agents therein are the people of God.

The canons (Title I, Canon 6) mandate that:

> ...each congregation shall be established according to the state's or jurisdiction's laws, handle its own finances, and carry insurance coverage in amounts specified by its diocese.

Additionally, Canon 6, Section 5, specifically concerns governing boards, and it states that each congregation:

> ...shall have a governing board, often known as the vestry, which is chosen and serves according to applicable laws, diocesan canons, and the congregational by-laws. The Presbyter in charge of the congregation shall always be a

member of the governing board and its presiding officer except as provided by the diocesan canon. The governing board is responsible for the temporalities of the congregation and, except where otherwise provided by canon, supports the clergy in the spiritual leadership of the congregation.

Notice that the canons of the Province spell out the purpose of a vestry or governing board. We will examine this later in the book, but this canon is a good summary. In terms of leadership, there are legal areas, financial areas, and fiduciary responsibilities that need attention in the local congregation. The vestry gives leadership and attention to these and other areas.

It would be worthwhile for the vestry to fully understand the canonical duties associated with its role at the level of your diocesan canons. You can likely find the governing canons of your diocese on the diocesan website, and these are important documents to be aware of for your work together.

Again, the canons of the wider body trump the canons of the smaller body. This means that if there is a conflict between the diocesan canons and the parish by-laws, the diocesan canons take precedence.

THE CHURCH'S GUARDRAILS

Canons are the church's guardrails, allowing us to see our freedom and boundaries. When the rector and vestry align with these canons, the church can achieve harmony and health. We can go anywhere we want within the framework of the canons. But the canons do not allow us to go everywhere we want.

This is good news for your vestry and the mission of your congregation. It means that your church is independent in discovering a local expression of Christ's mission, but your church depends on the linkage to your bishop and diocesan family. Your church is free to be the congregation you are called to be or become, but you are not free to do anything you want. There is local authority in developing your mission and regional accountability in carrying it out.

With this understanding of canons, let's discuss the local congregation's culture. Churches can be either congregational or hierarchical, but the size of the congregation is the most significant factor in determining the church's operations and governance. Membership size and average Sunday attendance (ASA) are key indicators of this.

As we dive into the roles and responsibilities of the rector, vestry, and bishop, we must first consider the congregation's size, which greatly influences the church's culture and governance. Stay tuned as we explore this important aspect in the next chapter.

---

1. Quote from an address to the Anglican Communion Network, 2005.
2. See the Appendix for a list of canons that every vestry member should know.

CHAPTER 4

BIG CHURCH, SMALL CHURCH

CULTURE, SIZE, AND LEADERSHIP
MUST ALL MATCH

Large or small, a church's governance should empower clergy and laity to work together to accomplish God's mission.[1]

— N.T. WRIGHT, ANGLICAN BISHOP AND
THEOLOGIAN

When it comes to church size, one model does not fit all—understanding your congregation's culture is key. The dynamics between rector, vestry, and congregation shift dramatically depending on church size and culture.

In terms of governance, hierarchical churches are characterized by a top-down approach. They have a well-defined hierarchy of clergy, with bishops or other judicatories at the top, followed by priests or pastors, and then deacons. Those in higher positions of authority make decisions, and the structure is designed to promote uniformity and consistency across the entire organization. On the other hand, congregational churches are more decentralized, with authority resting in the hands of the congregation as a whole. Members have a say in decision-making processes and the direction of the church.

However, the size of a church can significantly impact its ability to achieve its mission. Larger churches often have more resources and can leverage economies of scale to accomplish more. They may have larger budgets for outreach and evangelism and can afford to hire more staff to support their ministries.

As we all know, a church's size does not always indicate its success or impact. Small churches can be nimble and adaptable, able to respond quickly to the needs of their communities. They may have closer relationships with their members and a stronger sense of community.

As we consider the role of the rector and the vestry, however, we must look at the size of the congregation.

FOUR SIZES OF CHURCHES

We can draw parallels from the education sector to understand the leadership dynamics of churches of different sizes. I propose a typology that considers four unique types of schools, their learning environments, relative size, and makeup. By examining these different contexts, we can identify distinct patterns and cultures that can be applied to the local church.

The first context is the home school, which typically has few students and a single teacher. This can be seen in small, intimate congregations where the rector plays a significant role in all aspects of the church's life, from worship to administration.

The second context is the grade school, which has a larger student body and a team of teachers who each specialize in different subjects. This can be seen in mid-sized congregations where the rector still plays a central role but is supported by a team of lay leaders who oversee specific ministries, such as music or outreach.

The third context is the high school, which has an even larger student body and more specialized teachers who each focus on a specific subject area. This can be seen in larger congregations where the rector oversees a staff of associate clergy and lay leaders with a particular area of responsibility.

Finally, the fourth context is the college, the largest and most complex of the four contexts. A college campus has multiple schools and departments, each with its own faculty, staff, and leadership structure. In the church, this can be seen in mega-churches and dioceses, where the rector or bishop oversees a vast network of clergy and lay leaders who work across multiple locations and ministries.

By understanding the unique dynamics of each context, we can identify principles that can be applied to the local church. For example, in a home-school-style church, the pastor may need a hands-on approach and be involved in all aspects of the church's life. In a grade school-style church, the rector may need to delegate responsibility to a team of lay leaders overseeing specific ministry areas. In a high school-style church, the rector may need to lead a staff of associate clergy and lay leaders with particular expertise. In a college-style church, the rector or bishop may need to oversee a complex network of clergy and lay leaders who work across multiple locations and ministries.

Let's get into some specifics and see how this "school typology" can help us understand the role of the rector and vestry.

. . .

THE HOME SCHOOL CHURCH

Do you know anyone who homeschools their children? There is a distinct size and culture dimension in that learning environment. Learning occurs in a living room or around a kitchen table. A home school is a loving, learning, and training center for children, protecting them from larger institutions' challenges. The home school is a place of nurture.

Now, consider this culture as it applies to a congregation. The home school-size church has an average Sunday attendance of about 20-40. Everyone does everything together. The vestry is elected rather informally, and after a while, all of the adults in this size church are expected to serve on the vestry. Everyone should have a turn at it. A vestry member may be in charge of a specific church task, the way a family puts together a household chores list. Hopefully, there is great joy and community in this size congregation. The rector knows everyone, and there is access to the pastor or rector in the same way every student in the home school can find the teacher/parent. The rector's spouse and children are well-involved in this size church.

In a small church like this, a vestry might meet and talk about last week's lower-than-normal attendance like this: "I know the Smiths and the Garnets were both vacationing this weekend," says one member. Another says, "Well, Betty has been ill, and Wilma has a mother to care for now. I guess that's why they weren't in church. That's two more families out." The pastor says, "I heard Arnold's car broke down on Saturday afternoon. He called me on Sunday to see if I could find a ride for him, but it went straight to voicemail. He would bring his four kids, so that is another half-dozen people down."

This size church is going to remind most people of a family. Families are great when they function well. New visitors to this type of family church see a group of people who are super friendly to each other. However, there might be a downside to this size church. The home school-size churches can sometimes seem closed to outsiders. Entrance and acceptance into this kind of church may take a long time.

It is easy to see the appeal of a home-school-size congregation. They are one big happy family (hopefully).

THE GRADE SCHOOL CHURCH

In most communities, there are Grade Schools or Elementary Schools. The Grade School classroom is much more structured and standardized than the Home School environment. There is one primary teacher in the classroom, and perhaps teacher's aides who volunteer their time. The single teacher is responsible for all knowledge transmitted and permitted in the classroom.

Some churches correspond to this kind of culture. These churches have about 50 to 80 people in attendance. The rector is the purveyor of information and the organizer of all curricula. He oversees each member's learning and provides instruction appropriate to their age and stage in life. The rector of the grade school-size church is most appropriately called "Father." In this size church, the "Father Knows Best," if you recall the old television show. He is the one who always says, in a loud voice, "The Lord be with you," to bring people to attention. All shared meals begin with his prayer. Few meetings ever happen without his presence.

This type of learning environment can also be very nurturing. I can remember the name and the face of every single one of my teachers in grade school. They have imprinted their names and faces on me that I still recall after nearly 60 years! Mrs. Stephens, Mrs. Flotow, Miss Waddell, and Mr. Ezzo. All of them are in my mind's eye. By contrast, I remember only a few of my high school teachers.

There are obvious challenges for the sustainability of this size church, and this is a widespread problem for many congregations in the ACNA. These churches may have great fellowship and family strength, but they have a hard time growing past the ability of the one leader to be the "father" for more than 80 people.

THE HIGH SCHOOL CHURCH

So now, let's consider the next size church category as a high school. This is a church of about 100–200 people. Looking at this size as a school, we see it is not organized around a person. It is organized by subject. Students no longer have one primary teacher facilitating knowledge in each subject. Instead, they have a team of specialists and teachers. Students have several teachers to learn from, but they can still have their favorite teacher. The high school setting provides a broader opportunity to develop school spirit and identity, extracurricular activities, and a clear organizational culture.

The rectors of a high school-size church can rightly think of themselves as high school principals in many ways. The rector here is a leader of leaders. If a science teacher is absent one day from the classroom, you would never expect the principal to teach science that day or any day. You'd expect the principal to develop a system for absentee teachers to find a substitute and provide a daily lesson plan.

In this size church, if the youth pastor resigns, you would never expect the rector to lead the youth group for the next few months until another youth minister is hired. Additionally, people usually attend this church not because it has a great rector who tirelessly tends to the needs of the people. They attend the church because they have heard it has a great youth program, a thriving overseas mission program, or a robust small group program. It reaches the community around it by offering ministries and ways that people can be trained, engaged, and involved.

The rector or "principal" is the person who hires and interacts with department heads on the one hand and leads and reports to an administrative board (vestry) on the other hand. Indeed, the vestry of this size of a church feels more like a board of advice and counsel, which is appropriate. In this church, there is a greater emphasis on communication and coordination.

As we should begin to imagine, various churches of different sizes employ different methods to accomplish their objectives and create their programs. In the previous chapter, we looked at three kinds of churches according to their size. Most of the churches in the ACNA fit into these first three categories. In this chapter, we will look briefly at the largest church in our denomination and then pose some practical ways to tell what kind of church your congregation best represents.

The College Church

The fourth size church in the typology is the college-sized church. It might be a smaller college-sized church of 400 to 800 or a large university-sized church of 1000 people or more. Churches of this size are their own institution and are very rare. There are very few of these churches in the ACNA.

These churches have their own culture, ethos, and ecosystem. They are well-known to the broader community and their peers and have a particular reputation, for better or worse. The rector leads like a college president, with different departments or schools having their own internal structures. Most of the rector's work is with the faculty and governing board. The board is probably a group of alumni and experts recruited or persuaded to serve. The vestry of a church this size may be similar. Some members will be highly involved, others will love and value the church, while still others bring specific skill sets. The glue that holds a parish of this size together is individual parishioners in small groups or class experiences, as well as those who participate in the large public events of worship and celebration. Preaching and music are key reasons why many people attend this church, even if they have no other connection point.

In this size church, you first hear the word "campus." The buildings and facilities receive far more attention at this stage. A college president might be building their campus constantly, figuring out what is needed and which departments need more room, supplies, etc. Rectors and vestry members should expect facilities to be a significant part of their leadership dynamic at this stage of growth. They also have greater levels of financial responsibility, which need appropriate accountability and controls.

WHICH CHURCH ARE YOU?

Is your church the homeschool model, the grade school, the high school, or the college? It might be a function of size and more of a function of the local community's culture and the temperament of the leader (rector) and board (vestry). The kind of typology your congregation resembles will also have a lot to do with the culture around you, the size of the community where you live, and the kind of churches already in your community.

There is a way to find out what kind of school/church you attend. Remember last week's part of the Sunday morning service standard to every church: The Announcements. What was said? Who said it? What did they talk about?

You know the drill. At some point in the service, before, middle, or after, someone tells everyone else the essential things to know about the church as the week, months, or seasons roll on. Imagine that "Announcement" moment in each of these four churches.

The Homeschool Church Announcement

The leader stands up at the time of the announcements and says, "Good morning. I can see most of us made it today. I know it's cold outside, but thankfully, Betty has plugged in the coffee pot. It will be hot when we are through with our service." There is a pause while the leader looks over some notes, then turns to one of the most tenured members and says, "Bill, did you want to say anything about the upcoming parish meeting?" Bill makes his announcement and then sits down. The priest says, "Okay, well, let's talk about who is in the hospital and who needs our prayers this week."

The Grade School Church Announcement

The rector stands up and says, "Good morning. I tried to greet you all as you came into church this morning, but don't take it personally if I didn't. I'll be at the back of the church to shake your hand on your way out." There is a slight pause before he continues. "I am starting a Bible study for men this weekend and looking forward to it. We have had a few sign-ups, but we could use more men to join us. But it is not a boring Bible study, men. We are having a Cornhole Tournament afterward—and I have been practicing!" There is another slight pause. "Oh, one more thing, we are getting some youth here occasionally. If you have any experience leading teenagers, I need your help. I am committed to reaching the youth of our community. Please talk to Linda after the service if you can help or know someone who can." Linda is his wife and the mother of their two teenagers.

.   .   .

THE HIGH SCHOOL CHURCH ANNOUNCEMENT

The Rector or the Associate Rector stands up before the congregation and says, "Good morning. You can read all about our programs and activities in your bulletin this morning and on the website. We have lots going on for the new people to join! But today, we have some great news about our upcoming mission trip. We are leaving in two weeks, and I want you to meet Frank and Stacy Miller, who have organized it. Frank is the coach for our Men's softball team, and Stacy is on staff here part-time. They are organizing the whole thing. Please welcome them as they come up and tell us more about the trip ahead and how you can support it with prayer and finances."

THE COLLEGE CHURCH ANNOUNCEMENT

The Executive Pastor stands before the church body and says, "Good morning. I'm glad we have all our programs and announcements in the booklet in your pews. Please take one home to keep on your kitchen table. Your entire family will find things happening in our church just for them. But today, I want to remind you that our Rector has a clear vision about our relationship to the wider community. We want to get to know and serve them in any way we can. This morning, we have invited the Chief of Police to come and share some of the things that are happening around us and how our church can be involved through prayer, support, and service to help the men and women in blue. Let's welcome Chief Williams up to have a word with us." The Chief comes forward in uniform to a resounding amount of applause.

I HOPE THESE FOUR VIGNETTES HAVE BEEN A HELPFUL way to see how a church operates within its own culture and size.

Each has a unique 'vibe,' and mixing them would be very awkward. Could a small Home School church invite the Chief of Police in uniform? Yes, but it's not likely, and it could be awkward. Could you imagine a staff leader in a College-size church telling interested youth volunteers to talk to a person named Linda? Who is Linda?

Do you like this metaphor? There is another way it is helpful. Think about the role of the rector in each of these categories. In the Home School Church, the Rector is a chaplain to the family. In the Grade School Church, the Rector's role is like a Father of the family. In the High School Church, the Rector is a Coach. And in the large College Size Church, the Rector is more like a Mayor.

A church comprises not only the Body of Christ but also a group of individuals and programs working collectively to advance the mission of the church and the Gospel of Jesus Christ. Various churches of different sizes employ different methods to accomplish their objectives and create their programs.

The WEDCAP model offers a useful approach for vestries and the rector to comprehensively assess their program and ministry. Before we delve into the responsibilities and duties of the rector, vestry, and bishop, let us explore a method to manage, improve, and expand programs that promote the church's mission.

---

1. Quote from his essay "The Future of the Anglican Church," published in *The Anglican Communion at a Crossroads: The Future of Global Anglicanism,* 2019.

Worship
Weekly Services,
Inspiration & Hope

External Focus
Service, Outreach,
Mission

Discipleship
Teaching, Small Groups

Communications
Branding, Marketing,
Informing

Administration
Buildings, Grounds,
Vestry, Finances

Pastoral Care
Provision & Care

© THE REV. CANON DAVID H. ROSEBERRY

CHAPTER 5

INSIDE THE MISSION-DRIVEN CHURCH

HOW WORSHIP, EVANGELISM, DISCIPLESHIP, COMMUNICATION, ADMINISTRATION, AND PASTORAL CARE FIT TOGETHER

The Church exists by mission, just as a fire exists by burning. Where there is no mission, there is no Church.[1]

— EMIL BRUNNER, SWISS THEOLOGIAN

The new vestry person might remember their first meeting as a vestry. They may have been overwhelmed with the number of programs, events, on-campus activities, and gatherings a church has every week. It can be overwhelming.

A typical church organizes various programs regularly to serve its congregation and community. These may include Sunday worship services, Bible studies, Sunday school classes, youth group activities, women's and men's ministries, prayer meetings, fellowship events, and potluck dinners. Other programs may include outreach and evangelism efforts such as mission trips, community service projects, and vacation Bible school programs. Many churches also offer counseling services, support groups, and pastoral care for members in need. Music ministries, choirs, and worship teams are common in churches, children's ministries, vacation Bible school programs, and summer camps. Some churches also offer classes on finances, parenting, and marriage enrichment, while others may host recovery programs, addiction support groups, or job training initiatives. Finally, many churches have active social media accounts, websites, and podcasts, offering resources and opportunities for members to connect and grow in their faith.

Whew!

But how are these programs to be organized, evaluated, supported, and promoted? In this chapter, I want to employ a comprehensive template that will organize every program and activity of a church into a department or category so that the vestry and the rector can see everything they are doing—and see it all at once.

WEDCAP: AN ORGANIZATIONAL PLAN FOR MINISTRY

In my experience as a church planter and rector, I have developed a method for understanding a congregation's various programs, leadership, dynamics, and practices. This model is called WEDCAP, an acronym for Worship, External Focus/Evangelism, Discipleship, Communication, Administration, and Pastoral Connection. As I stayed at Christ Church in Plano for over 31 years and saw the church grow through all four stages of church size—Home School, Grade School, High School, and College—I saw how effective a simple system can be in understanding the adult ministry and programs of a local church.

WORSHIP: WEEKLY SERVICES, INSPIRATION AND HOPE

Worship is central to our faith and forms the foundation of every congregation. A comprehensive infrastructure supports each congregation's worship life, with various roles and activities contributing to the overall experience.

Every program, plan, offering, organization, infrastructure, and schedule would be part of this system of Worship. This would include all the staff whose assignments fall into this function. Every time the people of God gather and worship with music, communion, prayer, ushers, greeters, altar guild members, acolytes, or social moments afterward, these functions are understood as part of the church's worship life.

Worship is not only about singing praises and praying together; it's also about creating a space where people can encounter God and experience His presence. This involves careful planning and coordination of various elements, including the choice of songs, the preparation of the worship space, and the facilitation of an atmosphere conducive to worship.

In addition to regular weekly services, a congregation's worship life may include special events like prayer vigils, healing services, or seasonal celebrations like Easter and Christmas. These events provide opportunities for the church community to come together in a focused and intentional way, deepening their relationship with God and one another.

External Focus: Service, Outreach, and Mission

The external focus or evangelistic outreach system directs a congregation's focus outward, ensuring the church remains engaged with the broader community. Its primary purpose is to respond to Jesus' Great Commission to "go" and make disciples, teaching them to obey His commands.

However, this system is more than just about performing good deeds. While churches can certainly work to improve their communities, the ultimate goal of evangelistic outreach is to share the Gospel and lead people to Christ. This requires a delicate balance between serving others and proclaiming the Good News.

To accomplish this, churches should develop outreach programs tailored to the needs of their communities. This might involve partnering with local schools or organizations, hosting events for the neighborhood, or providing resources to those in need. Throughout these efforts, it's essential to maintain an evangelistic focus, seeking opportunities to share the Gospel in both word and deed.

If the church is engaged in outreach efforts that draw people to the church—such as Alpha, Marriage Enrichment, Parenting, or

Financial Budgeting for Families—all of these are in the Evangelism system.

Evangelistic outreach also involves cultivating relationships with non-believers. Church members should be encouraged to invite friends, neighbors, and coworkers to church events or services, fostering genuine connections that can lead to opportunities for sharing their faith. By maintaining a consistent and intentional evangelistic presence, the church can make a lasting impact on the lives of individuals and the community as a whole.

DISCIPLESHIP: TEACHING AND SMALL GROUPS

Discipleship training is an essential aspect of church life, providing a framework for nurturing spiritual growth and maturity in believers. While teaching imparts knowledge of the Bible and church doctrines, discipleship focuses on actively training individuals to practice their faith in daily life.

A robust discipleship program offers a variety of opportunities for learning and growth, including adult Sunday School classes, Bible studies, workshops, and small group meetings. These gatherings allow believers to delve deeper into Scripture, ask questions, and engage in meaningful discussions about faith and life.

I think we all would admit that most training courses and teaching curricula in the modern church are offered for children. In many congregations, there are fewer programs for adults than for children. This seems backward. Jesus blessed and cared for children, but he taught and trained adults. Today, we do the opposite. And we are weaker because of it.

Of course, in addition to adult discipleship, churches must also prioritize the spiritual development of children and youth. This involves creating age-appropriate programs that introduce young people to the Bible, help them build a relationship with Jesus, and equip them to navigate the challenges of living out their faith in a secular world.

COMMUNICATIONS: BRANDING, MARKETING, INFORMING

The fourth area in this system is the intricate web of communication channels that a congregation weaves internally and externally. Encompassing weekly newsletters, Sunday announcements, bulletin inserts, written blurbs, social media posts, and website information, these strands of communication form a circulatory system of knowledge, ensuring that each congregation member remains well-informed of ongoing events.

Many congregations fall prey to the "one-and-done" approach, in which a solitary Sunday morning announcement by the pastor is presumed sufficient. This strategy is flawed on multiple fronts. First, it overlooks that a considerable portion of the congregation may be absent, often around 70%. Second, the human propensity for selective attention means that even those who are physically present may not truly absorb the message.

Therefore, the best communication ministries understand the need for redundancy and reiteration in communicating anything important. And only some things are important. *A rule of thumb in church work is that being very efficient is not very effective.* The most efficient form of communication is speech. We can say things easily and quickly; the spoken word is free. It is *very* efficient. But simply telling a group of people something is not effective.

In real terms, effective communication requires repeated repetition and redundant reiteration, along with written words, posters, graphics, signage, emails, letters, testimonies, web pages, and collateral artwork posted at strategic places around the church. You are right if you read that last sentence and think about how much it costs to get a message out; how inefficient it is to have to create a congregation-wide communication campaign just to relay a message that everyone should understand simply by telling them. It *is* inefficient. But that is what makes it effective.

ADMINISTRATION: BUILDINGS, GROUNDS, VESTRY, AND FINANCES

The fifth pillar of a congregation is its administration—a domain as unassuming as essential. The administrative core encompasses mundane yet critical tasks like counting and spending money, setting up chairs, paying utility bills, deciding on policies, addressing human resources issues, establishing budgets, and balancing financial books. Boring? Perhaps. Crucial? Undoubtedly.

Rarely do individuals join a church because of its stellar administrative systems; however, faulty or dysfunctional systems can certainly drive them away. Trust and integrity in managing finances and budgets are paramount, as congregants will only donate according to their faith in the organization's reliability.

This area of church life would include the vestry, all buildings and grounds, the staff benefits and human resources, contracts, insurance, and financial accounting. The vestry plays a crucial role in the administration. They should not meddle in the nitty-gritty of discipleship training or worship, nor should they attempt to control evangelistic outreach. Their mission is not to fix the church but to govern and nurture its development.

PASTORAL CARE: PROVISION AND CARE

The sixth and final element of a church is the pastoral care and connection system, which fosters a sense of family within the congregation. This is where most ministers find their calling: to serve the Lord and His people through personal ministry, including baptisms, counseling, weddings, funerals, hospital visits, home visits, and casual meetups.

It is often the pastoral connections that draw individuals to a particular church. They feel seen, valued, and supported by the pastor and staff. However, the friendships and connections forged within the congregation keep them there. The need for a sense of belonging and community within the church is vital.

Even larger churches, which may appear impersonal and unfriendly to outsiders, can foster warmth and connection among their members. They become large precisely because they have found ways to create smaller, intimate communities within the larger congregation.

The pastor cannot maintain a deeply personal connection with every congregant, but most people only require such a connection in times of crisis or significant life events. It is during these moments that the pastoral touch becomes invaluable.

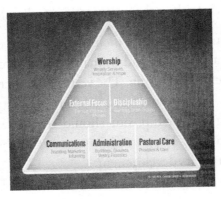

The WEDCAP Model for Mission

WEDCAP: THE BIG PICTURE

When these six systems are arranged in a triangle, they give an accurate picture of the common life of any parish. (See a full-page rendering of this triangle at the end of this chapter.)

WORSHIP

The top place is given to Worship because that is the main reason why a church exists.

EVANGELISM AND DISCIPLESHIP

The second and third sections cover the congregation's entire adult programming and ministry. Evangelism and Discipleship are like the twin engines of the airplane. They keep the church flying and moving forward. The bottom three spots are more 'under the radar.'

COMMUNICATION, ADMINISTRATION, PASTORAL CARE

The various channels for communication are transparent to most members—they don't join a church because of its great website.

The same is true with administration. People don't pay attention to sound administration practices and policies until the policies fail or there is some question about financial accounting. Then everyone is interested.

And finally, the pastoral care connections that clergy and ministers make are more informal, personal, and spontaneous. They are an essential part of the life of a church, but those touches—counseling, bereavement, pastoral care—are not church programs.

These six components form the intricate tapestry of every Anglican congregation. While some may have a unique seventh element or perhaps only five systems, the good news is that there are not 10–12 systems to manage.

SO WHAT?

But what value does this list hold? Why is it crucial to identify these six components? The answers to these questions have far-reaching implications for the vitality and health of your congregation.

Consider these six elements as a lens through which to examine your church. It is all too easy to look at the multitude of programs and activities taking place and feel a sense of pride. We might think, "We are an active church; who wouldn't want to join us?" However, if the clergy, staff, and vestry were to analyze their congregation through the framework of these six systems, they might gain a new understanding. This six-element lens can illuminate areas where resources are spread too thin and require further development.

They can and should be actively interested in helping the rector achieve excellence in the church's worship life. They must allow and budget for proper communication methods in the parish. They should also maintain the church's commitment to evangelism, discipleship, worship, and pastoral care. Each category needs to be made strong for the church to thrive.

THE VESTRY GETS AN "A" FOR ADMINISTRATION

As we will see later, *the primary place the vestry should "live" is in the Administration section.* If you scan ahead in this book to see the vestry's role, you will quickly see that the vestry has its hands full. They cannot and should not try to control or determine the functions of worship, discipleship, evangelism, and the host of other activities mentioned earlier in the chapter. The primary area where the vestry should locate their activity is under the "A" in the WEDCAP model: Administration.

If you read this and serve on the vestry, you might see this as a demotion. You never signed up to help with the Administration of the church, but I would encourage you to think of Administration as one of the most essential systems of the congregation. It is hard to separate it out, just as it would be difficult to separate out the nervous or skeletal system in the human body. The vestry's task is critical to the life and health of a congregation. But its role is primarily Administrative in the broadest sense of the word.

TO ILLUSTRATE: THE LIBRARY BOARD

Here is a clarifying illustration:

My father-in-law served faithfully on the local library board. He loved it, and they loved him. He loved to read, and he read voraciously. He cared about helping children to read more. He helped to raise the funds to put a small garden in the back of the library building. He went to library board meetings eager to help promote reading, books, and literature in his community. For a time, he served as assistant treasurer for the library and represented the library to the town council when they asked for information.

But my father-in-law was not a librarian. He did not know one thing about the Dewey Decimal System. He was keen on computerizing the entire library but knew he knew nothing about computers or how it would work. His attendance at the monthly library board was a regular part of his personal schedule, but so was his weekly trip to the stacks, where he would find new books to borrow and read at home.

He never thought that being on the library board meant he was suddenly in charge of the library.

There was a competent and trained librarian in that role. If you had asked him what he did for the library, he would say he helped it fulfill its mission. Was his role primarily administrative? Yes! And look at all that he could do under that single heading! He was both a reader and an administrative leader on the board.

So, in applying the analogy to the local congregation, it follows that a vestry member's main activity should not be direct creation or oversight of a program or ministry of Worship or Discipleship. They can and should have an active interest and investment in these areas, but the vestry should look to the rector for leadership. The rector should look for ideas, interest, passion, and participation from the vestry. The rector should also rely upon the vestry to provide feedback and guidance, but the congregation members should not expect the vestry to take over the Worship life of the church.

Typically, the vestry might assume they are elected to help run the church services and oversee the congregational life in all its expressions. This is a difficult task, but it is simply impossible for a rotating group of elected volunteers to meet for 2–3 hours a month. This is not in their wheelhouse—this is the rector's job. In an attempt to do this, to manage all these programs and systems, most vestries will frustrate the rector and volunteers and gum up the system.

The rector's role is to foster health and spiritual strength in each of the six areas. As mentioned, the rector may involve vestry members for their advice or counsel. He may create a task force to look into an area and help him see reality more clearly. A rector can bring up any topic or point of discussion at a vestry meeting. Conversely, a vestry member should be encouraged to ask questions at a vestry meeting. However, suppose the rector was to ask a vestry member to "fix" a Discipleship program, for example, or "take charge of the newsletter" (Communication). In that case, he is asking the vestry member to take on a staff function. This system approach to looking at the entirety of the congregation is a helpful way to see the church as a whole. And, like the human body, the healthier each of the systems is, the healthier the whole of the body is.

NOW THAT WE HAVE FRAMED THE ISSUES AND THE culture determined by size, we can look at the roles of the rector, wardens, and the vestry in the following chapters. We will also have some important things to say about the role and the relationship that the diocesan bishop has with the parish through the rector and the vestry. Each role will find its expression within the culture of its specific church.

---

1. Quote from his book *The Word and the World*, 1931.

RECAP: LOOKING BACK ON OUR FOUNDATIONS

The local Anglican church is a unique organism with many interconnected parts that must work harmoniously to fulfill its God-given mission. As we have explored, the size and culture of a congregation significantly impact how it is structured and governed. Homeschool-sized churches operate like close families, grade school-sized churches are led by a central father figure, high school-sized churches function through specialized ministries and staff, and college-sized churches resemble multifaceted campuses. Each model presents distinct opportunities and challenges for leadership and administration.

Every church, regardless of its present form or leadership structure, should be attentive to the following priorities as it carries out its work:

1. Maintain a fervent commitment to worship as your fundamental reason for being, creating environments where people can encounter the living God. Structure

your worship services with excellence, artistry, and spiritual depth that draw people into His presence.

2. Keep evangelism central by consistently offering outreach programs tailored to your community. Balance demonstrating God's compassion with clearly communicating the Gospel message in word and deed.

3. Make discipleship a non-negotiable priority by providing multifaceted teaching and training opportunities. Pursue spiritual growth and biblical literacy among all age groups, especially adults.

4. Commit to proactive, redundant communication that ensures vital information circulates efficiently to the entire congregation. Recognize that being strategic with messaging is more valuable than being sparse.

5. Value administration by building trust through responsible institutional leadership, financial management, and administrative competence. Prevent problems and confusion by putting sound policies and procedures in place.

6. Foster pastoral connections within the congregation through members caring for each other in times of crisis and celebration. Create smaller communities within the larger body to nurture belonging and relationships.

When held in partnership, the six areas in the WEDCAP model allow churches to thrive in their unique settings.

As we conclude this section, we should remind ourselves that the church is the embodiment of Jesus on earth. This transcendent purpose defines the local church. While methods and models may vary, every congregation shares a common calling to incarnate the loving, liberating, transforming way of Christ within its own community and context.

By God's grace, your church has been entrusted with this vocation. As we will see in the next section, the rector gives visionary leadership to these foundational ministries. The vestry governs the structures that empower such ministries. And the bishop upholds the apostolic DNA that animates each local congregation. Clarity surrounding these symbiotic roles and systems will enable your church to flourish in its next season of ministry and mission.

In the next section of the book, we will define the unique roles of the rector, the vestry, and the bishop.

CHAPTER 6

THE ROLE OF THE RECTOR
DUTIES THAT ONLY THE RECTOR CAN DO

The rector bears the cure of souls in a parish and is responsible for worship, teaching, and pastoral care.[1]

— RICHARD HOOKER, ANGLICAN PRIEST AND THEOLOGIAN

The following canon comes from the Constitutions and Canons of the Anglican Church in North America. It establishes that rectors, clergy, and their roles and responsibilities fall under the authority of their bishop and diocese. At its core, the canon mandates that every congregation must have a rector, acting rector, or priest-in-charge shepherding the flock under the supervision of a bishop.

Norms for the calling, duties, and support of rectors and other Clergy and the dissolution of a pastoral relation shall be provided by each diocese. Rectors shall be domiciled in the diocese to which their congregation belongs.

— —*TITLE III, CANON 7 - OF RECTORS AND OTHER CONGREGATIONAL CLERGY*

Notably, while affirming a rector's leadership, the canon defers to diocesan bodies in defining the rector's duties, nodding to the autonomy of congregations and dioceses. In other words, the diocese, not the national body, determines the roles, responsibilities, and duties of the rector in their diocese.

Therefore, it is impossible to spell out a common set of specific roles and responsibilities for the rector of a congregation. The canons of the Province and each diocese determine the standards under which rectors and other clergy function. However, it is safe to say that all diocesan canons have a common understanding. No priest has carte blanche to lead their congregation however they want. Their bishop is truly their overseer.

However, from a governance overview, we can say this much: the vestry collaborates with the rector in the temporal and spiritual leadership of the congregation. It is also clear that the rector has a unique level of autonomy under the bishop's direction—especially in the parish's vision, worship, and program life. Also, the rector is part of the governing board and serves as its presiding officer. This gives us canonical clarity, but what does it look like in practice? Let's look at the five duties of the rector.

The list below summarizes those duties that belong to the rector exclusively and cannot be delegated to other priests on staff.

THE FIVE DUTIES OF THE RECTOR

The following overview of the roles of the rector comes from my years of experience as a rector and my observations from working with congregations. My overview is only my opinion. It does not have the weight of a Canon at all. But whatever wisdom I might share with you on this subject is born of experience and conversation with many other rectors.

1. LEAD TOWARD THE VISION

The role of the rector in a parish is essential in articulating and developing the stated vision of the church. The rector is tasked with preaching, teaching, interpreting, upholding, exemplifying, shaping, and developing the vision and mission of the congregation. Whether it is contained in a formal mission statement or not, the rector must become the principal spokesperson in communicating and leading the congregation toward the vision.

Having a great vision or idea for the future is not sufficient. As the leader, the rector's responsibility is to guide and inspire others toward a biblical and Gospel-centered vision. The rector's main task is to constantly communicate how God has used and is currently using His people to further the Gospel. In simpler words, the rector should work to lead the congregation forward on the church's mission. A significant part of the rector's work is to remind, reflect, remember, and reiterate the congregation's direction toward its mission.

The term "vision" can be interpreted in many ways, and for the rector's role, it is commonly mentioned that the rector should "cast the vision." However, this phrase has been used so frequently that it has lost its significance. In the following chapter, we will explore in greater depth what it means for the rector to "cast a vision." For now, it is enough to say that the rector's primary and most vital role is to lead. By providing guidance and direction, the rector assists the congregation in focusing its energy and resources on fulfilling its mission and advancing the Gospel of Jesus Christ.

In the next chapter, we will discuss this idea thoroughly. The rector should be the CVO, the Chief Visionary Officer. And we will look at the specific duties it entails.

2. BUILD THE MINISTRY TEAM

The rector should not be a Lone Ranger. If there is a vision that can be articulated, the rector should build a team of people who can help move the church to fulfill that purpose. There are groups and committees and staff, whether paid or volunteers, who need the rector's voice and touch on a routine basis. However, the vestry is one of the groups that act as servant leaders and help the parish's vision become a reality.

As Anglicans, we value clean lines and godly order. Here, the line is clear. The rector oversees the team. Oversight of the teams or ministries is not the role of the vestry or any liaison from the vestry. This is an important distinction because often, the rector sees the vestry as adjunct staff or liaison committee leaders. If desired, the rector can make that assignment, but the point remains the same. It is the rector who oversees the committee or the group.

This is what is meant by the Latin phrase, *ex officio*, or "from the office" of the rector. A rector is an ex officio member of every guild, group, committee, task force, or team in the parish. This means that, through the Office of the Rector, a rector is on every team, guild, or group regardless of whether they are present for the meeting.

It is important to note that the rector should not be required, or even expected, to attend every meeting of every committee, chapter, program, function, or guild in the congregation. This ensures that a rector has complete control over the program and processes that make a church function. If I put this privilege another way, it might sound more pointed: The rector is always welcome to attend, participate, direct, or disband any group within the parish.

But why should the rector have this kind of availability and involvement in every church program, committee, chapter, function, or guild? Should the rector be a perpetual busybody or a control freak demanding that everything and everyone falls in line with the vision?

Remember the WEDCAP model mentioned earlier. These six divisions represent everything that is going on in the congregation. A rector should be virtually omnipresent because the rector's duty is to bring spiritual health and vitality to *every* part of the congregation. The rector is to be the "chief spiritual nutritionist" for the entire congregation.

There is usually flexibility in the dynamic of this reality based on church size (which we talked about in Chapter Four), but the point holds that the rector gives oversight and management.

3. Provide Spiritual Leadership

The rector has a unique leadership role in the area of shepherding. They are to provide for the people. There are many things the people need (some of them, they even want!) that the rector should make sure they receive: pastoral care, meaningful worship, gospel-centered programs, sound teaching, clear communication, sound administration, marriage preparation, community engagement, outreach ministry, deployment in mission, prayerful counsel, and so much more. The rector doesn't do all of these things, but the rector ensures these are provided for in the parish.

Returning to the WEDCAP model for a moment, the rector should assume responsibility for developing health and spiritual rigor in all six areas of congregational life. This is the role of spiritual leadership, and the rector is the only one who can or should embrace it. Their role is to ensure that the people are cared for authentically and appropriately. The rector should ask, "What do these people of God need to grow more committed to the Lord and His Gospel and to become more sensitive and obedient to the leading of the Holy Spirit?"

The rector seeks to provide the answer to that question.

4. MAINTAIN PERSONAL ACCOUNTABILITY

Providing spiritual leadership for the people requires that a rector understand how to lead themselves. This is difficult because it involves seeing the congregation from a subjective point of view—to love, protect, and provide for them and to care for and nurture them in the Lord. But at the same time, the rector must also be an objective leader and ask critical questions about their commitment to the church's mission. Are the people disengaged? Are they apathetic? How can they be awakened and challenged?

These are the same questions every leader needs to ask themselves: Have I become lazy or inert in my faith? How can I develop or deepen my devotion to the Lord?

To this end, it is interesting to note that the rector and all priests and deacons are *not* members of the congregation they serve. Very few people know this, but it is canonically true. The priests and rectors are members of the diocese, where they are canonically resident. They are held accountable to the bishop for the health and strength of the church they serve and for their spiritual life.

There is an old joke about a newly hired employee reviewing his job description after he begins his new assignment. He sees the acronym "ODAA" and wonders what it means. His boss smiles and finally tells him the truth about his workload. It means "Other Duties as Assigned."

Indeed, there are many duties that the rector has beyond the usual list of responsibilities in a so-called "position description" (this is what makes evaluating the rector's performance a challenging thing to do). Every day is different. The rector may have four pastoral meetings in one day and no meeting for the next four days. The rector doesn't punch a clock. They don't report their hours to a boss. Hours are spent every day for which they are unaccountable to anyone.

And still, the rector feels the burden of the spiritual welfare and well-being of the congregation. This is why the rector must have self-leadership, as mentioned earlier. They must know when to tend to their spouse and marriage, protect Sabbath time, seek counseling or spiritual direction, or engage a leadership coach.

Each rector must be self-aware to know when to set the burden down and get rest, perspective, and refreshment. A pattern is all too often repeated. Burnout is very real, and a rector will know they are burned out on the inside long before it is evident on the outside.

5. Develop and Steward Resources

Raising money is only one way for the rector to develop and steward the congregation's resources. The rector should also take stock of the congregation and its many assets, abilities, and accomplishments and put them to use for the Kingdom of God. How are disciples made and trained in this congregation? How do churches get planted through the congregation? How can the congregation support the seminary and seriously encourage young people to enter seminary training and leadership? How is the diocesan fellowship of the clergy or the Province blessed because of the congregation's resources, people, and staff? In other words, how can God use the people and programs of the congregation to expand the church?

The rector is responsible for stewardship of everything in and of the parish. Of course, this means money, but it means so much more than money. To be a steward of the parish, in this sense, is to be a custodian of the people, property, and opportunity the congregation has to further the Gospel. The rector is responsible for how the parish is fully aware of the mission it is called to engage. This is a privilege for a priest to undertake as a rector, but no one should doubt the gravity of the task or the weight of the responsibility.

And, of course, raising the financial resources to do the work of the parish is a significant part of the rector's stewardship role. It means that the rector is in charge of raising the money to supply the resources for the congregation. They must have a biblically developed confidence to raise the financial resources needed while simultaneously giving the congregation the discipleship opportunity to grow in generosity.

The vestry can help in this area but is not the primary fundraiser. The buck stops, or rather starts, with the rector. Helping the congregation understand the biblical use of money, articulating a theology of stewardship, and challenging people to give is one of the most rewarding and impactful things a rector can do, and only the rector can do it.

But this work cannot be done by the rector alone. Indeed, in many churches, the vestry assumes this role. But that is not a wise course of action. The rector has the spiritual authority and the logistical ability to organize and develop a communication and teaching plan for stewardship. The vestry should overwhelmingly support the stewardship program of the rector.

In summary, the rector's role is vital to a congregation's health and direction. As the chief spiritual leader, the rector is uniquely tasked with articulating and embodying the church's vision, building a ministry team, providing pastoral care and theological guidance, maintaining personal spiritual accountability, and stewarding the church's resources. Though the specific duties may vary across contexts, the rector is generally responsible for oversight of worship, discipleship, evangelism, ministry programs, and administration.

The rector collaborates with the vestry in governing the parish but has a distinctive leadership role in setting the spiritual tone. By preaching, teaching, and modeling the way forward, the rector helps the congregation live out its mission. The role requires prayerful dependence on God, self-awareness, people skills, spiritual depth, and administrative gifts.

When exercised well by a prayerful, discerning rector, it can significantly strengthen a church's impact for Christ. The role is weighty but essential—and offers the blessing of helping guide God's people in the way of Jesus as well as lead the people to a vital relationship with him.

---

1. From *Of the Laws of Ecclesiastical Polity*, 1594

CHAPTER 7

THE RECTOR AS CHIEF VISIONARY OFFICER
A TRUCK DRIVER AND A SERVANT LEADER

Servant leadership recognizes that the leader's authority comes not from power, control or institutional office, but through the freely-given consent of followers.[1]

— STEPHEN PICKARD, ANGLICAN PRIEST AND THEOLOGIAN

I f your Bishop formally installed the Rector of your parish, chances are they prayed this prayer or one with similar intentions and sentiment. Read through this prayer carefully.

O Lord my God, I am not worthy to have you come under my roof; yet you have called your servant to stand in your house, and to serve at your altar. To you and to your service I devote myself, body, soul, and spirit. Fill my memory with the record of your mighty works; enlighten my understanding with the light of your Holy Spirit; and may all the desires of my heart and will center in what you would have me do. Make me an instrument of your salvation for the people entrusted to my care and grant that I may faithfully preach the Gospel and administer your holy Sacraments, and by my life and teaching set forth your true and living Word. Be always with me in carrying out the duties of my ministry. In prayer, quicken my devotion; in praises, heighten my love and gratitude; in preaching, give me readiness of thought and expression; in worship, increase my zeal for godly preparation; and grant that, by the clearness and brightness of your holy Word, all the world may be drawn into your blessed kingdom. All this I ask for the sake of your Son our Savior Jesus Christ. Amen.

It is easy to see why the rector needs to have a steady life of prayer and why the rector needs to be prayed for and prayed with regularly. This is a heavy load.

I would add one more duty for the rector that only the rector can fulfill. The rector is called to be the CVO—the Chief Visionary Office of the Congregation. The rector casts the vision.

But what does it mean to "cast a vision"? As I mentioned in the previous chapter, the phrase is overworn, in my view. It has lost its meaning, and it would be good to reimagine what it should be. So, let's look at how the rector can and should be the chief visionary for the congregation.

THE RECTOR IS A TRUCK DRIVER

If a picture is worth a thousand words, a metaphor—a word picture—is worth a thousand pictures. Therefore, I'd like to provide a metaphor to help explain the role of the rector within the church. This image can help rectors, vestries, and congregations alike to comprehend the rector's multiple responsibilities.

Imagine the rector as a truck driver, perhaps of a Toyota Tacoma, or "Taco" as they're called in Texas. Just as a driver needs a clear view of the road ahead, the rector must have a vision for the church's future. The rector's job is to look through the "windshield" and determine the church's direction. Think of Moses, who guided his people toward the Promised Land and described in detail what it would be like to live there:

For the LORD your God is bringing you into a good land, a land of brooks of water, of fountains and springs, flowing out in the valleys and hills, a land of wheat and barley, of vines and fig trees and pomegranates, a land of olive trees and honey, a land in which you will eat bread without scarcity, in which you will lack nothing, a land whose stones are iron, and out of whose hills you can dig copper. And you shall eat and be full, and you shall bless the LORD your God for the good land he has given you.

— DEUTERONOMY 8:7–10

Do you see what Moses is doing? He is showing people their future in a new land. He is giving them a picture of what is coming, particularly what is in it for them. He is explaining the faithfulness of God in terms they can understand. If you were to ask Moses to paint a picture of what was coming for them, he could do it! It is real. It is tangible. It is so vivid that the people will know what to look forward to. It is a vision worth going for.

Returning to the Taco Truck, there are four different elements of leading people into the future, into the vision. The rector exercises his role as CVO by answering four different questions.

WHERE ARE WE GOING? - ENVISIONING OUR FUTURE

As the "Rector" of the Hebrews, Moses saw the future more clearly than anyone else and took the time to convey it to the people following him. Likewise, the rector must have a clear vision for the church's future, inspiring and motivating the congregation. This vision should be rooted in the church's mission and values and encompass both short-term objectives and long-term aspirations. By articulating this vision effectively, the rector can empower the congregation to work together toward their shared goals.

WHERE HAVE WE BEEN? - LEARNING FROM OUR HISTORY

The rector's role includes reflecting on the church's past to understand better the journey they have been on and how it has shaped the congregation. This process requires the rector to facilitate open discussions, fostering an environment where the community can collectively examine their history, successes, and challenges and discern the lessons learned. By engaging in this thoughtful reflection, the church can grow stronger, deepen its faith, and be better prepared for the future.

WHAT DO WE NEED FOR THE JOURNEY? - PACKING RESOURCES AND SUPPLIES

Third, consider the truck's cargo space. Given the limited resources available, the rector is responsible for determining which programs and initiatives to prioritize. Like a truck, the church can only carry the essentials for the journey.

The rector must also discern what is essential for the church's journey, making strategic decisions about allocating resources and prioritizing initiatives. This involves working closely with staff and vestry members to assess the congregation's needs, the church's mission, and the impact on the broader community. By regularly evaluating ongoing programs and exploring new opportunities, the rector ensures that the church remains dynamic and responsive to changing circumstances, carrying only what is necessary to fulfill its mission.

Who is on the Journey? - Building a Team

Expanding on the analogy of the rector as a Taco truck driver, it's important to remember that the rector does not undertake this journey alone. Remember, many Tacos in Texas have King Cabs! There is room for others from the staff and vestry to join in the ride. These individuals offer valuable counsel, assist in watching for potential obstacles, and help the church move forward together.

The rector's leadership should emphasize collaboration and inclusion, recognizing that staff and vestry members bring unique perspectives, skills, and spiritual gifts to the table. By embracing a team-oriented approach, the rector fosters a sense of unity and shared ownership within the church leadership. This collaborative spirit encourages open dialogue, creative problem-solving, and mutual support, helping the church to better navigate challenges and embrace new opportunities that arise along the way.

THERE IS ONLY ONE RECTOR

When I think about the rector's role in the church's life, I want to add an obvious but important point. Just as there is only one driver for the truck, there is only one rector. There will always be people riding shotgun, as we used to say in Arizona. There will be people in the backseat. There might even be folks under the hood, as it were. But there is and should only be one rector.

This bears a bit more emphasis. Churches are filled with all kinds of people doing all sorts of wonderful things. There is a myriad of teachers. Several clergy members may be on staff as associate or assistant priests. The church might have an ordained deacon or two. Multiple priests, deacons, and even bishops can work in the parish ministry. There can be other ordained leaders who preach sermons from time to time and lead worship regularly. There are wardens and vestry members, volunteers, and workers. But there is only one rector.

If an assisting priest is scheduled to teach or preach at a service but is somehow delayed or stuck in traffic, another priest or layperson can teach, preach, or lead. That is true of a youth minister, deacon, or staff person. But it is not true of a rector. Every church requires vision-defining leadership; only one person can provide it: the rector.

Put another way, many of the ODAA can (and should be) delegated to others, but decisive leadership is not one of them. The rector is like Moses, who leads the way, clearly describing the future in the best and most vivid language available.

A SERVANT LEADER

It's important to note that the rector is not a ruler and should never act in a bullheaded, stubborn, or autocratic manner. Instead, the rector should seek wise, honest counsel from trusted advisors. Leadership is a sacred charge that must be carefully managed, and the rector should always be aware of the potential for abuse or mishandling of this responsibility.

The rector should surround themself with individuals who are willing to speak truthfully and openly and who can provide valuable insight into the potential impact of any decisions that may be made. The rector must be willing to listen to this counsel and should be willing to reconsider or delay decisions based on pushback from trusted leaders.

It's vital for the rector to engage in thoughtful discussion, discernment, prayer, and collaboration when introducing new ideas to the vestry. Rushing decisions through without proper consideration can lead to unintended consequences. People need to test the leader's ideas, no matter how gifted or well-intentioned they may be.

One of the most important lessons for any rector is this: *people love change but do not like to be changed.* Wise words, indeed. Recognizing this truth, the rector should partner with the vestry and other leaders to foster a spirit of shared ownership and responsibility.

GIFTING AND GROWING

A healthy relationship between the rector and the vestry involves a dynamic balance of collaboration, communication, and respect. When the rector and the vestry work together effectively, the church can thrive and grow, meeting the needs of its members and the broader community.

As a church consultant, I often see parishes struggling to find this balance. When the rector and vestry can successfully navigate these challenges, the church can flourish. Each party should recognize and affirm each other's gifts and insights, and together, they should prayerfully seek the Lord's guidance for their congregation.

THE RECTOR HAS A UNIQUE AND VITAL ROLE WITHIN THE church, pointing to the future vision, interpreting the past, and providing for the journey. Yet, the rector does not undertake this task alone. The vestry serves as an essential partners, offering counsel, support, and prayer. Through this collaborative approach, the rector, vestry, and congregation can work together to create a vibrant and flourishing faith community.

---

1. Pickard, Stephen. "Leadership in the Anglican Tradition." In *The Oxford Handbook of Anglican Studies*, edited by Mark D. Chapman, et al., Oxford University Press, 2015.

CHAPTER 8

THE ROLE OF THE VESTRY
WHAT IT ISN'T AND ITS FIVE DUTIES

The vestry shares responsibility with the rector to guard the spiritual tone and unity of the congregation.[1]

— DR. MARION HATCHETT, LITURGICAL
SCHOLAR

As we begin exploring the role of the vestry in this chapter, it is helpful first to clarify what the vestry is not. Many clergy and laity come from denominations or traditions where they served on different governing bodies, like boards or sessions. With varied prior experiences, assumptions may exist about what the vestry is and does. To provide clarity, I want to highlight key differences by outlining what the vestry is not:

An Elder Board

Many people are familiar with a model of church governance where qualified spiritual leaders are appointed to lead and pastor the congregation. Usually, this is a non-rotating leadership position. While we certainly want spiritually mature leaders on the vestry, our system is not an "appointment for life" model. The rector is the one who has tenure, not members of the vestry.

A Board of Deacons

In many congregational types of church governance, the deacon board does a lot of the practical work of the church. The deacons are not "Deacons" in the Anglican "ordained" sense. No bishop has been involved in their ordination. They are, instead, the serving arm of the church. In our polity, the vestry serves the church but isn't simply a workforce.

Assisting or Adjunct Staff

In some churches, vestry members assume they are to "do" the church's work by running programs or teaching courses. Sometimes, a vestry member can be assigned as the point of contact with a particular program. It may work well to have different vestry members support specific ministries. Still, this system falls short of ideal, if for only one reason: the vestry is a rotating group of people coming on and going off the vestry every three years.

Keep in mind the vestry members are elected to their positions irrespective of whatever gifts they have. Staff members are called to their roles according to their gifts and abilities. In other words, it is not a foregone conclusion that every vestry person will have the gifts needed to also serve in a staff role.

. . .

CONSTITUENT ADVOCATES

Vestry members are not representatives of a particular constituency. They should not be nominated or elected because they are from the youth group or the altar guild or have an allegiance to a specific style of worship or service time. They should not advocate for one group or another. Their deliberation and consideration must take in the whole of the congregation.

THE FIVE DUTIES OF THE VESTRY

So, what is unique about the vestry? What does the vestry do that only the vestry is called to do? As I mentioned above regarding the role of the rector, I do not have a canonical warrant for all of these, per se. That is, I cannot point to a specific Canon or by-law that dictates these five roles, but I can say with certainty that these five areas MUST be attended to.

1. PROTECT THE VISION OF THE CHURCH

The vestry's primary role, in my experience, is to protect the stated vision of the church. Each vestry member should know the congregation's overall goals and visionary direction. The vision of a congregation is like a North Star. It is a fixed point of reference that is "out there." It helps the entire congregation orient their efforts and develop their program with respect to this vision.

The vision of a church should not change over time. It might be forgotten over a period of instability or vacant leadership, but a church should not adopt a new idea for a vision every few years. If the rector is newly elected or the church has transitioned to a new location or merged with another congregation, remembering and recalibrating around a new vision is good.

In an Anglican church, the vestry leadership rotates every year. It is usually against the diocesan canons to serve more than two consecutive three-year terms. Thus, there will always be a change in the vestry. New members will be elected each year, while other veterans will complete their term of service. Added to this change, there is an occasional transition of a rector. All of this turnover presents a challenge to the congregation; they can forget who they are and what they are trying to accomplish.

This challenge is all the more reason why a vestry should know and follow a clear vision year by year, season after season.

2. Support the Program and Plans

Alongside protecting the vision of a congregation, the vestry should help the rector develop effective methods or means to fulfill the vision. These are the congregation's plans, resources, and programs to pursue its vision. The vision is like a North Star and sets the church's direction. The programs are the way the church moves forward. These programs usually do not change quickly or easily, but they should be evaluated on a routine basis.

Let's look at an example. One church I consulted with worked, prayed, and, after some serious discernment and discussion, arrived at a clear vision of what God was calling their church to do. They were called to worship God, follow Christ, and go in mission to the outside world. This vision statement was based on multiple passages from Scripture, and their vestry and staff truly owned it.

But when they were finished, they were concerned that the statement never articulated how and what they wanted to do. This is where the "methods and means" come in. These are the actual ways a church actively decides to do and then does. They began to make decisions and choices and arrived at four main actions they would pursue. They would focus and build their Worship Attendance, Small Group Discipleship, Neighborhood Evangelism, and Overseas Mission to a specific area of the world. These were the four distinctive methods by which they would pursue their vision.

Let me cite another example. A few years ago, I worked with a medium-sized congregation that proudly boasted that they had over 18 programs where members and visitors could "turn their faith into action."

The congregation boasted that they were dedicated to the mission of Christ "by all means possible." I remember one meeting when I helped them count up the volunteers necessary to lead these programs. We discovered that several vestry members were in charge of multiple programs. They also realized that many people in the church were involved in multiple programs at the same time. But even more church members were not involved in anything! The activity was a "false positive."

They cut their programming by 60%, focused on only a few vital choices, and a year later, the church had grown. They did more by doing less.

A rector and vestry need to ask this question constantly: *We say we have a vision, so what are the methods and means by which we are pursuing it? Are the few programs that we have adequately staffed and funded? Are we expecting to have results from these means and methods?*

This is one reason the vestry must guard against getting swamped in the day-to-day operations of the parish and the details of running the church. If they lose the bigger picture of the purpose and goals, they will not have the perspective to help the rector see the mission field clearly. The vestry members work to build up, maintain, and ensure the means and methods align to pursue the vision. Mission clarity and well-funded means are vital areas of vestry leadership.

3. DEMONSTRATE LEADERSHIP IN FINANCIAL STEWARDSHIP

THE VESTRY MEMBERS HAVE ANOTHER VITAL ROLE IN the life of their congregation. They should exhibit and model the life of a generous steward over what God has entrusted to them. Of course, the vestry needs to oversee the financial resources of their church, but they also need to be responsible overseers of their own financial household. In my view, it is fair for those nominated to serve on the vestry to be challenged to be generous stewards and give abundantly to the church's ministry. They should recognize that the biblical tithe, while not a legal obligation, is the standard of Christian generosity. Is this standard respected? Is tithing a family goal?

Why is this important? Generous people who practice Christian stewardship are open-handed with God's money because they have seen God move in their financial lives in extraordinary ways. People who have not learned the joy of being a steward in their lives will find their tenure on the vestry filled with anxiety and worry.

It is also an issue of personal integrity. In attempting to teach and preach the Christian standard of generosity, the rector should have the confidence and assurance that the vestry is behind them. It is awkward for the vestry to expect the congregation's membership to be more generous than the members of the governing body themselves.

Of course, the life of a vestry leader involves oversight of the church's financial positions. One of the non-negotiable roles of the vestry is to protect the financial integrity of the church. The vestry should examine the financial reports monthly through a designated finance team (and appointed treasurer to lead that team). They should provide an annual accounting of all funds and work with the rector to develop the annual budget. They should be active in approving any long-term financial contracts or capital investments. They are fiduciary guardians of the financial life of the congregation to ensure that the church has a long-term future and is operating in a trustworthy way with all funds that have been generously given or responsibly borrowed. These items are spelled out in the next chapter and the Appendix.

While this role and responsibility belong to the vestry, in my experience, a Finance Committee should be appointed and charged to prepare a monthly overview for the vestry's information. If the vestry oversees the minutiae or details of the Finance Committee, it will get bogged down.

This Canon (I.9, Sec. 3) from the Province spells out the duties this way.

Financial responsibility and accountability are the obligations of the Church at every level... Every Diocese shall provide standards for record-keeping, financial accountability, insurance, investments, and the bonding of financial officers for both the Diocese and its congregations and missions.

The vestry should be aware of these standards and how they are spelled out in the canons for the diocese so that they can conform their practices, at a minimum, to those of the diocese.

4. SUPPORT THE RECTOR AS SPIRITUAL LEADER

The rector leads the way for the congregation in vision, values, and the stewardship life of the church. The vestry helps the rector and supports this work. There is a delicate, working balance. The vestry should never simply rubber stamp what the rector advocates, especially regarding the temporal matters of the church. They should represent the parish and the best interests of all the parish. This means they should not be "devil's advocates" or a counterbalance for the rector.

As mentioned above, the vestry members should not represent a constituency or their personal agenda. They shouldn't represent a particular interest group or specific program in the church.

This is not as easy as it sounds. People are very passionate about their faith and their church. We would all hope they would be. The vestry's role should include being a clear sounding board for the rector and learning to give honest feedback. However, a vestry cannot be divided on important issues, at least for long, and divisions or differences of opinion must be worked out and/or ameliorated by wise counsel and clear teaching. If there is sustained conflict between the vestry and the rector, the bishop's guidance and/or intervention may be needed.

Conflict is not uncommon in the church. We know this from the first pages of the Early Church in the Book of Acts. I cannot address this issue fully here. I honestly do not feel qualified, but many in our Anglican Church are. I want to make an important point about one kind of conflict: theological.

A vestry is not a theological body; they are not set up for theological deliberation. Certainly, most members serving on a vestry are not qualified to argue a theological or biblical point of view. These kinds of discussions are common in more "elder-led" congregational churches, but the Anglican hierarchical church governance structure is not suited for it.

This does not mean there cannot be biblical teaching, spirited discussion, and theological debate. But in the Anglican system, the vestry is suited for governance, not theology. Suppose there is a need to settle a theological dispute or solve a biblical issue. In that case, both the vestry and the rector should invite the bishop to attend their meeting, mediate the concern, and, if needed, render his opinion. It should be noted that if the bishop renders his opinion in a formal sense (written), the matter is considered settled.

The vestry is elected to support the rector and not to change their theology or the theology of the church. This doesn't mean that there has to be 100% agreement about key ecclesiastical issues (such as, for example, the ordination of women to the priesthood or the meaning of the Holy Eucharist). However, it does mean that the vestry forum is not the place to settle these issues.

5. PROVIDE FOR SUCCESSION OF THE RECTOR

The vestry plays a critical role in ensuring the future success of the church by planning for succession, which should be among its top five roles. This means that the vestry should have policies and by-laws in place to guide the process of finding a new rector in the event that the current rector resigns or departs.

It's important to understand that the rector of a church has a tenured position, which may come as a surprise to some vestry members. The rector's tenure is granted at a formal installation service conducted by the bishop, typically soon after the rector begins their duties. This means that the rector will hold their position until they resign or retire or are removed by the bishop in the case of a moral failure.

Given the certainty that a new rector will be needed at some point, the vestry must prepare for this eventuality. It's not a matter of if but when, and the vestry must be ready to act when the time comes.

Take note of this subject in the pages of the Appendix.

TO ILLUSTRATE: BATMAN AND ROBIN

If you wonder what kind of relationship the rector and the vestry should have, look no further than DC Comics. The Dynamic Duo, as they were called in Gotham City, functioned as a crime-fighting team. To develop this metaphor, let me refer to the very first Batman show I can remember. The original television series 1966 was so bad, cheesy, campy, and over-acted that it was legendary. What person my age doesn't remember it?

Batman and Robin had a shared mission. But we all knew that the Caped Crusader was out in front. He led the way; the Caped Crusader was in charge. The two action heroes each had different skills and strengths that complemented each other. They had strong communication between the two. They were frequently conversing and seemed to plan things together in the Batcave. They were both collaborators on what needed to happen next. And most importantly, there was a high level of trust between them.

So shall it be with the rector and the vestry. They are like Batman and Robin.

I have been a coach and consultant to more than a few rectors, vestries, and the relationship between the two. I have come to see it as a sacred relationship that God uses to advance the church's work. But there are troubles in the relationship from time to time. To use the DC Comics illustration to describe these conflicts, I can list three main reasons why vestries and rectors have significant conflict.

. . .

THERE IS A ROLE REVERSAL

The vestry has assumed the role of Batman, and they are holding onto the levers of power and authority. They try to control the rector by refusing funds. They speak behind his back about what a lazy Robin he is. Sometimes, in the worse scenarios, they meet together as Batman and do not bother to tell Robin about the meeting. Sometimes, the role reversal is so complete that they attempt to fire Robin! This is not a good situation, and it often poisons the well for future rectors for decades to come.

THERE IS ROLE DENIAL

In this case, the rector (Batman) refuses the leadership role. He is not interested in building a team or driving a truck, to mix metaphors. Sometimes the rector does not have a vision, or he is borrowing a vision that he had at a previous church. He does not involve the vestry. He doesn't lead the church. He steers it by himself. This is also a fatal flaw.

A NEW KIND OF HERO ARRIVES

In this case, the rector has abandoned the partnership metaphor completely. Instead, they have embraced another action hero from the DC Comics universe. He or she fancies themselves as Superman, able to do most important or impossible feats alone. They don't build a team. They don't consult or collaborate. This kind of rector just pushes their way forward with a stronger-than-steel frame.

IT IS TIME TO LEAVE THE WORLD OF COMICS AND RETURN to the real role and function of the office of the rector and the ministry of the vestry. However, it would be good to consider these metaphors when working together as rector and vestry. Have fun!

---

1. Quote from *Commentary on the American Prayer Book*, 1980

CHAPTER 9

THE VESTRY AND FINANCIAL OVERSIGHT

MONEY, ACCOUNTABILITY, AND TRUST

A church's finances should be managed with integrity, transparency and accountability.[1]

— THE REV. JOHN R. W. STOTT

Every vestry is responsible for the financial well-being of the congregation. No matter the size or dynamics of the parish, managing its finances is a critical responsibility that requires the vestry's attention. As stewards of the gifts that God has entrusted us through His people's generosity, we must exercise wisdom, prudence, and integrity in everything we do.

While vestry members don't need to be professional bankers or accountants, they must possess a basic level of financial competence to lead in this area effectively. It may be necessary for the vestry and/or rector to undergo additional training to enhance their skills. Sloppy financial management, or worse, malfeasance, is akin to having a rotten trellis: it will ultimately lead to disaster for the congregation. It could expose the rector and vestry to legal liability. Therefore, sound administrative leadership and processes are critical for financial accountability and transparency.

One of the key duties of the vestry is to appoint a treasurer who will work closely with the designated finance committee and any staff members responsible for financial matters. This position requires a higher level of expertise in financial management. In addition to appointing a treasurer, the vestry must pay close attention to financial protocols and oversight to ensure the parish's good health. This is not just a matter of doing business as usual—it is an integral part of the spiritual leadership of the parish. The vestry must understand the basics of cash position, cash flow, fund-raising, and church trends. The rector must also be actively involved in this process and work closely with the vestry on financial matters.

PROVIDING FINANCIAL OVERSIGHT

The monthly vestry meeting should include a financial report, and the annual budget should be a part of the vestry's yearly cycle of work. At a minimum, the vestry should receive two essential pieces of information each month - a balance sheet reflecting the current cash position, assets, and liabilities of the parish and a profit/loss statement (by account) for the previous month. These reports are crucial for monitoring the financial health of the parish. It's important to note that some vestry members may be more familiar with these reports than others. Therefore, I recommend that the vestry receives a basic orientation and refreshment of these concepts at least once a year, especially when new members join. The vestry is responsible for ongoing monitoring and annual oversight of the finances.

Preparing an operating budget is a key annual step for the vestry. It's the responsibility of the vestry to adopt the annual budget by a vote. The same budget, perhaps in summary form, should be presented to the congregation as part of an annual report or meeting. It is important to note that the congregation does not vote to approve the budget. They are free to ask questions, seek clarification, or question allocations, but the congregation is not a voting body. In fact, as we will say later, a congregation's only vote is to elect their vestry. The vestry votes for everything else.

Vestry members should understand a unique reality common among churches. Namely, that there are thirteen months in a year! This is because while expenses occur in twelve months, income is spread over thirteen months, with December accounting for about two months. This may be unnerving for new vestry members (and most treasurers!) who may feel that their church is going underwater month by month.

It's important to understand that churches typically receive money at a slower rate than they spend it. While many expenses are constant and predictable throughout the year, money comes in very unevenly. Some months are "lighter" than others, and the last month of the year sees a significant increase in giving. Rectors and the vestry must understand historical giving patterns and cash flow dynamics to avoid misunderstanding.

PROTECTING THE FINANCIAL CONDITION

The vestry should have a financial audit of its books regularly. I realize that a signed audit by a professional CPA is an expensive budget item. There are ways of reducing the cost of an audit by scheduling it during an off-season for a CPA firm or even performing it every other year.

Did you know that there are "lesser" audits that accounting firms can perform? I am not an accountant by any means, but I know the vestry should take a very careful look at the methods for handling cash and setting in place some serious safeguards. Sometimes, a volunteer or retired CPA in the parish might perform an informal audit.

The vestry should also have a report of the church's financial condition on a month-to-month basis. They do not need to have an in-depth analysis of the giving or spending trends in the church. Most financial reports should be limited to a single page and take about 20 minutes to read. A treasurer or a warden can cover the high (or low) points in that space and time.

This does not mean that the vestry would want to have only cursory reviews of the financial life of the church. A review group or financial committee should help review the accounts at a granular level. If the entire vestry gets into the weeds on financial items, they will disappear into those details and lose the big picture.

Again, the vestry should review the parish finances, but they should be listed on a single page, and a monthly report should not take more than 20 minutes.

The rector should maintain an "arm's length" approach to the financial reporting, counting, and distribution of funds. Therefore, the rector should never be the one to present the financial report to the vestry. They should always be present to answer questions and/or give assurances. And their role in the parish should be to maintain spiritual integrity even when it comes to the financial knowledge of what members give.[2]

Other than as a liturgical gesture, the rector should never handle the offering at a worship service. This is an internal check to safeguard the rector and the vestry. Imagine that a new church member or visitor sees that a priest of the church comes to the altar table at the end of a worship service and removes the offering plate, carrying it to an undisclosed location. Other people, such as an usher, altar guild member, or administrative assistant, should be assigned this task.

The offering given during a worship service should be immediately placed in a lockable deposit bag and stored until the next opportunity for it to be counted and recorded. The counting of the offering should never be done by only one person and never by the same two people week after week.

Most churches are close-knit collections of people who love and trust one another. Nevertheless, it is incumbent upon the vestry to develop and maintain clear safeguards against any malfeasance or even the appearance of casual financial management.

MAINTAINING TRUST OF MEMBERS, DONORS, AND COMMUNITY

Maintaining the trust of members, donors, and the community requires sound financial protocols. The vestry must know how money is handled, who handles it, who writes checks, and who approves expenditures. While the answers to these questions will differ from parish to parish, the vestry has a fiduciary responsibility to ensure that money is handled properly. Financial protocols, especially internal controls, should comply with parish bylaws, diocesan policies, and state guidelines. At a minimum, the vestry should know the basic chain of custody for how the offering is collected, counted, and deposited. Multiple people should be involved in this process. All protocols and methods are developed as a matter of good, sound business practices and are not personal.

Nothing I have written or included here should be construed as legal or financial advice. However, as I close out this chapter, I want to offer a few additional thoughts.

Your Members Love Your Church

It is probably true that everyone in your church wants your church to succeed. I think we have to assume that this is true in all churches. Every member will attend and support your church by choice. You are the best church they have found. They are committed to the complete health and vitality of your congregation.

This thought should be at the forefront of any person called to serve on the vestry. The members of your church want to be part of a congregation that makes a difference in the lives of its members and the surrounding community for the Lord.

I realize that we are all sinners in need of a Savior, and I recognize that some people want to serve on the vestry to harm the church, "correct" the rector, or change the service times for their own convenience. However, I have always believed that in a church, most people, for the most part, and most of the time, want to see their church thrive.

Your Members Trust the Rector and Vestry

The people who elect people to the vestry give it a high level of trust. They not only want their church to succeed, but they trust the vestry will help it to succeed.

This trust is the glue that binds people to the church's vision and its leaders. When people in the pews are called upon to pray for the church's future or to give for the church's future, they must have a deep trust in their leadership. They must have a deep conviction that people serving on the vestry can be trusted.

If members do not trust their rector or the leaders on the vestry, a church will circle its wagons and stall out. The congregation may be asked to give for a high-minded purpose, but if the people do not trust the leadership, the congregation will not respond.

This trust in the leadership is so special and vital to the organization that it must be vigilantly maintained year by year. Trust is critical to the movement of the church's mission, and if there is mistrust or broken trust, the movement will stop.

TRUST, ONCE BROKEN, IS LOST

Trust is a durable commodity between the vestry/rector and members until it is lost. Trust can quickly evaporate. Many people reading this book have served an organization that has suffered through the malfeasance of a board or the leader's fall due to the mismanagement of money. Sadly, it is not uncommon. We have all heard of situations where financial misdealing is discovered.

These three statements should form the framework for a few best practices to which the vestry and ordained leadership should hold fast. They may not all be doable right away, but at the very least, they should be seen as a goal for the church and its leadership.

Be advised: *The price of following financial safeguards might not be free, but the cost of not doing so could be astronomical.*

BEFORE LEAVING THIS SECTION OF THE ROLE AND responsibilities of the vestry, please be sure to read the chapter in the Appendix on the 10 Critical Areas of Oversight for the vestry.

---

1. Quote from his book *The Living Church: Convictions of a Lifelong Pastor,* 2007
2. This raises an issue that good rectors and vestries will disagree about. Should the rector have knowledge of what individual members contribute to the church. Personally, I think that knowledge is a vital piece of information for

the rector to have. So, I say yes. But I know that this opinion is not universal. It is beyond the scope of this book to deal with it thoroughly.

CHAPTER 10

THE BISHOP OF A DIOCESE
THE OFFICE AND ITS ORIGIN

The bishop is the chief pastor of the diocese. He is called to be a focus of unity and a guardian of the apostolic faith.[1]

— ROBERT RUNCIE, FORMER
ARCHBISHOP OF CANTERBURY

S o far, this book has focused on the dynamic and crucial relationship between the rector and the vestry. In many ways, a congregation's health and strength depend upon the health and stability of that relationship. But another person has a role in every Anglican Church, even when he's not around. This person might never attend a vestry meeting, but his presence is felt everywhere in the congregation. A few people might know this person, but he plays an outsized role in the spiritual life of every person in the congregation. This third person is the bishop.

Every Anglican congregation has a bishop. You cannot be an Anglican congregation without having a bishop. His role in the day-to-day life of the congregation is minimal, as it should be. But his influence and oversight are not. As the New Testament calls them, bishops are "overseers," which is the direct translation of the Greek word *episcopos*. In the following few chapters, I will describe the office of the bishop, its purpose and function, and how best to understand a healthy relationship between the rector and vestry and the bishop of the diocese.

But first, allow me to share a story that will demonstrate the importance and powerful influence of the office of the bishop.

THE OFFICE OF THE BISHOP

In 1982, I was ordained in the Episcopal Church. My wife and I relocated to North Dallas three years later to establish Christ Church. Due to the area's rapid growth, many individuals from across the country were drawn to our church. Our congregation thrived and displayed great potential and vitality. Throughout the following years, we established new congregations and constructed several buildings to accommodate the increasing number of attendees and members.

Meanwhile, the Episcopal Church was grappling with contentious debates surrounding human sexuality, scriptural authority, and the person of Jesus Christ. Active homosexuals were being ordained as deacons, priests, and bishops. The language in the liturgy of the Episcopal Church was shifting to gender-neutral pronouns in praying to God. God was no longer to be called "Father." Even Jesus' person and work came under scrutiny or suspicion. These issues would come to splinter the Episcopal Church and the Anglican Communion in the coming years. And Christ Church, through our vestry, decided to leave the Episcopal Church and join others to form the Anglican Church in North America.

As I reflect upon those difficult and tumultuous days, I see that the teaching role, pastoral authority, and importance of the office of bishop were at the center of this drama. From time to time, rectors and preachers in congregations have taught or promoted false doctrines, but by the nature of their individual platforms, they could never do system-wide damage. In other words, there have always been those who teach outside the boundaries of the Christian faith. But when bishops do it, they can do great harm because they have a vast platform and an outsized impact on the whole church.

BREAKING UP IS HARD TO DO

A bishop may not be seen on the campuses of the congregations in a diocese, but the preeminence of the role makes his teaching ever-present. He is installed as the Chief Pastor, Chief Teacher, and Chief Shepherd of an entire Diocese—both clergy and laity alike. He is the overseer. If his teaching is unorthodox or erroneous, the damage he can do to the minds, hearts, souls, and spirits of the people in his Diocese is incalculable.

Leaving the Episcopal Church was a costly decision in myriad ways. Relationships were severed. Personal reputations were besmirched. Large sums of money were paid out. Attorneys were involved. We lost some of our momentum for growth. Members of our church whom I had known since its inception left the congregation. It was a very sad time for me. I had been an Episcopalian all of my life. Our decision to leave was the right one, but I deeply regretted having to make it.

However, put succinctly, our congregation left the Episcopal Church because of our Anglican polity. To remain a faithful Anglican church under a faithful Anglican bishop, we had to leave our home denomination and form a new church, a new Province.

Effectively, we had to start from scratch and build a new denomination.

That is the crucial role and importance of the bishop.

DO WE NEED BISHOPS?

The story I have just told raises the question: Do we need them? Why not have a church without bishops? It is a good and fair question to ask, and tens of thousands of congregations have faithful and effective ministries without bishops. Are bishops a "need to have," or are they a "nice to have"? (An extended discussion of this distinction is beyond the scope of this book, but a summary of the arguments can be found in the Appendix.)

This is a question that the historic Anglican Church has wrestled with mightily. Even our great Anglican reformer, Thomas Cranmer, was not convinced of the need for a separate office of bishop.

In the first editions of the Book of Common Prayer (1549, 1552), in the spirit of the Reformation, the role of the bishop was downplayed—only two offices were needed in the church. But ten years and several monarchs later, under Elizabeth I, the 1662 Book of Common Prayer and Ordinal more firmly etched the three-fold order of ministries into Anglican practice and theology.

Cranmer's earlier Reformed views did not take lasting root. The prevailing Anglican ethos favored continuity with catholic order balanced with Protestant reforms. This resulted in the long-term reestablishment of bishops along with priests/presbyters and deacons that has characterized Anglicanism since.

Anglican polity asserts that the office of the bishop is critical to the fullness of the church. Why? Because, as Anglican polity asserts, bishops are the successors of the apostles. The apostles were appointed by Jesus Christ to be his witnesses and to continue his work after he ascended into heaven. Bishops are seen as the successors of the apostles because they continue the apostles' work by preaching the gospel, defending the faith, presiding in synods, and administering the essential rites of ordination and confirmation.

Thus, the bishops' teaching must be congruent with the Apostles' teaching.

WHERE BISHOPS COME FROM

We will focus on the role of bishops shortly, but now, let's look at the reason for bishops according to the Bible, the Book of Common Prayer, and the Canons of the Anglican Church in North America.

THE BIBLICAL MODEL OF BISHOPS

The Bible provides many passages in the early Christian Church that speak to the need for bishops, overseers, or shepherds. Here are a few examples:

> Keep watch over yourselves and all the flock of which the Holy Spirit has made you overseers. Be shepherds of the church of God, which he bought with his own blood.
>
> — ACTS 20:28

This passage, spoken by the apostle Paul to the elders of the church in Ephesus, emphasizes the responsibility of the overseers to watch over and care for the flock of believers and to lead them in a way that reflects the sacrifice of Christ.

Since an overseer manages God's household, he must be blameless—not overbearing, not quick-tempered, not given to drunkenness, not violent, not pursuing dishonest gain. Rather, he must be hospitable, one who loves what is good, who is self-controlled, upright, holy and disciplined. He must hold firmly to the trustworthy message as it has been taught, so that he can encourage others by sound doctrine and refute those who oppose it.

— TITUS 1:7-9

This passage, written by Paul to Titus, emphasizes the importance of overseers being upright and disciplined, holding to the sound doctrine of the faith, and being able to refute those who oppose it.

Be shepherds of God's flock that is under your care, watching over them—not because you must, but because you are willing, as God wants you to be; not pursuing dishonest gain, but eager to serve; not lording it over those entrusted to you, but being examples to the flock. And when the Chief Shepherd appears, you will receive the crown of glory that will never fade away.

— 1 PETER 5:2-4

This passage, written by Peter to the church elders, emphasizes the importance of overseers serving with humility and a willingness to care for the flock and the reward they will receive when Christ returns.

Overall, these and other passages in the Bible suggest that the need for bishops or overseers is rooted in the responsibility to care for and lead the community of believers, uphold the sound doctrine of the faith, and serve the people of the church with humility and self-lessness.

From the Book of Common Prayer

In the Book of Common Prayer (2019), deacons and priests receive ordination during a service that grants them the authority to conduct religious rites and ceremonies on behalf of the church. Once ordained, they remain priests or deacons for life. However, if an ordained priest is chosen to become a bishop, he undergoes a "consecration" ceremony that sets him apart for a sacred purpose. This does not change his ordination. He remains a priest and a deacon. Consecration as a bishop is not a promotion. It is a unique calling to a new kind of sacred ministry. The bishop is called and set aside to be a shepherd to his people, a teacher of the faith, and a leader in the church.

In the service of the Consecration of a Bishop, the Book of Common Prayer includes a section for the public examination of a candidate for bishop. This section lists the functions and duties to which the candidate must agree. The public, formal examination is designed to ensure that the candidate is willing to fulfill the responsibilities of the office. Here is the list of things to which the new bishop must agree to do:

- To believe that the Holy Scriptures contain everything necessary for salvation through faith in Jesus Christ.
- To instruct the people committed to their charge and to teach or maintain nothing necessary to eternal salvation but that which may be concluded and proved by the Scriptures.

- To faithfully study the Holy Scriptures, call upon God by prayer for their true understanding, use them to teach and exhort with wholesome doctrine, and to withstand and convince those who contradict it.
- To banish and drive away from the Church all erroneous and strange doctrines contrary to God's Word and to encourage others to do the same.
- To renounce all ungodliness and worldly lusts and to live a godly, righteous, and sober life as an example of good works.
- To maintain and set forward, as much as possible, quietness, love, and peace among all people, and to exercise such discipline as is committed to them by the authority of God's Word and the Order of the Church.
- To be faithful in examining, confirming, ordaining, and sending the people of God.
- To show oneself gentle and merciful, for Christ's sake, to poor and needy people and all strangers destitute of help.

This is a "job description" like no other in the church. All bishops need our prayers. And those of us who are not bishops—priests, deacons, and laity—should never forget the high calling of this office and help our bishops become the servant leaders we need.

According to the Constitution and Canons

The role and function of the bishop are also provided in the Constitution and Canons of the Anglican Church in North America, where a broad outline of the bishop's origin, purpose, and responsibilities is found.

Article I: Fundamental Declaration #4 states that "the godly historic Episcopate" is an inherent part of the apostolic faith and practice and is "integral to the fullness and unity of the Body of Christ."

Article IV asserts that the fundamental agency of mission in the Province is the local congregation and that the congregations and clergy are gathered together in a diocese or network and "united by a bishop." And in Title 3 and Canon 8, we are given a detailed description of the office of the bishop.

These duties can be summarized as follows:

- A bishop is called by God and the Church to be a shepherd who feeds and oversees the flock entrusted to his care.
- Bishops are consecrated for the whole Church and are successors of the Apostles through the grace of the Holy Spirit given to them.
- Bishops are chief missionaries and pastors, guardians and teachers of doctrine, and administrators of godly discipline and governance.

Bishops are chosen by a diocese in accordance with the constitution and canons of the diocese and must be approved by the College of Bishops with a two-thirds majority vote.

IN SUMMARY, THE BISHOP IS RESPONSIBLE FOR BRINGING together the congregations and clergy in a diocese or network and providing leadership. The bishop serves as a diocese representative, networks at the Provincial Council and Provincial Assembly, and acts as a Provincial College of Bishops member. The bishop also plays a crucial role in overseeing the diocese's governance, constitution, and canons or network, ensuring they align with the Constitution and Canons of the Province. Furthermore, the bishop may work with other dioceses towards a common goal or operate as a unique jurisdiction at the sub-provincial level.

I mentioned earlier that bishops carry enormous power and influence in their office because of their calling. But they cannot wield it like a sword or a club. They are called to be defenders, pastors, guardians, and shepherds. How should we understand the relationship between the rector, the vestry, and the bishop of a diocese? This is the area to which we turn next.

---

1. Source: "Authority in Crisis?"

CHAPTER 11

THE BISHOP AS GRANDFATHER

AN COMPELLING ILLUSTRATION, A PRINCIPLE, AND A CHALLENGE

Bishops are chiefly pastors called to exercise oversight, care and responsibility for the clergy and laity of the diocese.[1]

— MICHAEL RAMSEY, ARCHBISHOP OF CANTERBURY 1961-1974

To better understand the role of a bishop in a church, it is helpful to use a metaphor of three generations of the human family: a household, its parents, and a grandfather. In this metaphor, the congregation is like a household, the rector is like a parent, and the bishop is like the grandfather.[2] The grandfather's (bishop) love and concern extend to multiple households within a large family, providing wisdom, guidance, and support. He encourages and supports the parents (rector) of those households. The parent (rector) is responsible for the care, instruction, and welfare of a particular household (congregation).

Metaphors can be oversimplified, but let's play out this family model of relationships as it applies to the specific relationship between the bishop, the rector, and the congregation's vestry.

THE BISHOP AS GRANDFATHER

Like a grandfather with the parents, the bishop and rector maintain an open and active line of communication, respecting and deferring to each other's wisdom, experience, and spiritual authority. They are mutually supportive, working together in love and humility to further the Kingdom of God within the larger family.

Like a grandfather with the rest of the family, the bishop and the congregation connect through periodic visits, encouraging and teaching the family members and learning from their experiences, joys, and struggles. The elder's presence demonstrates unity and continuity within the church family.

And like the parents and the rest of the family, the rector and the vestry collaborate closely, sharing responsibilities and decision-making authority to actively care for and minister to the congregation's needs. Together, they steward resources, cultivate spiritual growth, and ensure the spiritual welfare of the congregation.

Each member of this family metaphor—the bishop as the grandfather, the rector as the parent, and the congregation as the household—holds a vital role in the Church's health, strength, and unity. As in a family, the relationships within the Church should be grounded in love, respect, trust, and collaboration.

What else can be said about these relationships according to the metaphor? In a healthy family:

- The grandfather/bishop is a valued member of the family and highly esteemed.

- He is typically seated in a place of honor at family gatherings and speaks as the custodian of the family's history and traditions.
- The parent/rector takes care of the household's day-to-day responsibilities and is loyal to the bishop, referring to him as a "Father in God."
- The grandfather's/bishop's influence is felt throughout the family through his supportive and respectful relationship with the parent/rector.
- He knows he cannot replace the parent/rector and should never interfere.

TO ILLUSTRATE: LESSONS OF THIS FAMILY FATHER

Allow an illustration to drive home the point.

When my children were young, my wife and I made all their decisions, including what they ate and wore and which doctors they visited. As they grew older, we gave them more independence to make their own choices. During their teenage years, we shared information about making choices and offered guidance to help them make good decisions and avoid bad ones.

When our children reached their twenties, we had to step back. They chose their own way, even if we didn't always agree with them. When they married, we had to step back even further, as they had a whole other set of in-laws and family traditions to consider. When they had their own children, we had to let go even more.

Our involvement in the day-to-day details of our grandchildren is minimal, even though we love and care about them very much. We offer advice only when asked, and when we are, we see it as an opportunity to show support and share our family values. Our primary focus is on investing time and energy into our relationship with them.

And so, the same can be true for interpersonal and diocesan relationships and roles of bishops, the rectors of congregations in a diocese, and the vestries of each church.

The metaphor of a multigenerational family is a helpful tool to imagine and describe the three-part connection between the bishop, the rector, and the vestry. It has been helpful.

But also, the metaphor is useful to illustrate a critical concept that the framers of the ACNA had in mind as they put together the founding documents for the Province. It is known as the principle of subsidiarity. We can use the metaphor again to make this concept clearer to us.

PRINCIPLE OF SUBSIDIARITY

The principle of subsidiarity is a political, economic, and ecclesiastical (church law) doctrine that holds that decisions should be made at the lowest level possible. The principle is a crucial pillar of the Anglican polity. In the Anglican tradition, decisions are made at the local level as much as possible. This means that the congregation makes decisions about the life of a congregation, the diocese makes decisions about the life of a diocese, and decisions about the life of the Province are made by the church as a whole.

As before, picture the Anglican Church as an extended family gathering, with the bishop as the respected grandfather, the rector as the responsible father, and the congregation as individual family households. Subsidiarity is a principle that guides this family-like structure, allowing smaller, local groups to make decisions that best suit their unique needs, much like how each family decides on house rules and in-house traditions.

The bishop is the chief pastor and leader of the diocese, but the bishop is not the dictator of the diocese. The bishop is called to assist and support the rector and the vestry in making decisions for the congregation's good.

The subsidiarity principle helps define the bishop's relationship with the rector and the vestry. But the principle also helps to define the bishop's relationship to the entire diocese as a whole. According to the tenets of subsidiarity, the bishop makes decisions for the diocese in consultation and relationship with the people of the diocese, who make decisions through their elected representatives, the rector, and the vestry.

It is important to note that the bishop of the diocese has the ultimate authority over matters related to worship, Prayer Book usage, and the maintenance of Church doctrine, discipline, and worship within the diocese.

THE CHALLENGE OF THE ORDINATION OF WOMEN

Although subsidiarity has its benefits, it can also pose some difficulties. When each parish has the freedom to make its own decisions, it can result in variations in how church teachings are understood and implemented. The same is true concerning a diocese. Subsidiarity can also lead to inefficiency and duplication of efforts, as separate parishes may work on the same projects without coordinating, wasting time and resources.

In the Anglican Church in North America, we can see the challenge of the principle of subsidiarity most clearly concerning the range of views about women's ordination to the priesthood.

The Anglican Church in North America (ACNA) has adopted the principle of subsidiarity, allowing individual dioceses to decide where they stand on the issue of women's ordination. This decision was made to promote autonomy and respect diverse perspectives. However, the decision has fostered ongoing tensions within the ACNA. Essentially, each diocese operates as its distinct brand with unique beliefs and practices. The Province even uses a phrase to describe this opinion, which is an oxymoron. Based on a resolution from the 1988 Lambeth Conference[3], the Province says it has "two integrities." But this is a contradiction in terms. "Integrity" is singular. But Scripture doesn't seem as clear on how to decide this issue as many wish it were.

This is the challenge of the principle of subsidiarity. Some dioceses will never assent to ordaining or even welcoming women as priests in their diocesan borders. Other dioceses ordain women as a regular part of their mission. Can these two dioceses continue to be in the same Province? How could they find common ground? And who would make these decisions?

Balancing subsidiarity and unity is delicate for the Church as it strives to accommodate diverse viewpoints while maintaining harmony and cohesion among members. Such balance enabled the foundation of the Anglican Church in North America. Thus, ongoing unity and fellowship will require dialogue, mutual respect, and a commitment to finding common ground while individual dioceses exercise autonomy within the broader church community.

---

1. Quote from his book *The Christian Priest Today*, 1972
2. I am using this metaphor to illustrate a relationship between three entities: congregation, rector, and bishop. This metaphor is used for illustrative purposes only and not to indicate gender roles. The Canons of the ACNA provide for bishops to all be men. But this does not apply to the role and office of rector.
3. The 1988 Lambeth Conference passed Resolution 8 stating that both positions regarding the ordination of women are held with integrity in the Anglican Communion. It acknowledged that this issue has led to division and impaired communion within provinces and between provinces.

CHAPTER 12

THE ROLE OF THE BISHOP

FIVE DUTIES, SEVEN TOOLS, AND THE COLOR PURPLE

Bishops are elected leaders who oversee clergy and congregations, carrying on the apostolic succession.[1]

— FROM THE CHICAGO-LAMBETH QUADRILATERAL, 1888 STATEMENT ON ANGLICAN IDENTITY

A s I am not a bishop, I have relied on the source documents mentioned earlier for guidance. Additionally, I have had the privilege of working under several bishops who, unbeknownst to them, served as excellent examples of what a bishop should be. Out of respect, I shared these five bullet points with numerous current bishops and welcomed their input.

It will be helpful if we see them as a list of five duties alongside the five responsibilities of the rector and vestry.

THE FIVE DUTIES OF THE BISHOP

To simplify the bishop's role and responsibilities, we can categorize them into five distinct but interconnected roles and duties. Rather than being completely separate from each other, these roles often represent different values or overlapping images that form a collection of the bishop's overall duties.

A Visible Sign

An Anglican bishop fills an important symbolic role, visibly representing Christ and the Church in many ways.

As he travels through the diocese, the bishop signifies the church's unity across diverse parishes and peoples. By participating in joint worship and shared service, he maintains bonds of fellowship amidst difference. The bishop makes unity in Christ tangibly evident.

In his teaching and way of life, the bishop upholds the apostolic tradition passed down through the centuries. Drawing on Scripture and Anglican heritage, he faithfully adheres to historic doctrine and practice. Yet, with wisdom, he adapts the tradition for modern contexts, avoiding rigid traditionalism.

The bishop also visibly signifies the divine grace available in the sacraments. By overseeing the proper administration of baptism, communion, and other rites, he guarantees channels for God's grace. His leadership of rich liturgy points people toward the transcendent.

The role of an Anglican bishop is essential for the life and mission of the church. The bishop is a visible symbol of the unity, apostolic tradition, sacraments, pastoral ministry, and mission of the church.

He is a role model for the people of the diocese and is called to live a life of faith, hope, and love.

DEFENDER OF THE FAITH

A bishop has an important responsibility to defend the faith within the church. This includes upholding orthodox teachings through preaching, writing, and theological discussion. Bishops must teach clearly on matters of doctrine, morality, and spirituality so that the faithful understand the tenets of their belief. They also preserve orthodoxy by combating heresy and error and disciplining clergy who contradict church teachings. By ordaining new leaders and resolving disputes, bishops promote unity and ensure the church remains in communion.

Beyond preserving internal orthodoxy, bishops have long engaged outside challenges to the faith. They advocate for the church in the public sphere and defend its teachings when controversial issues arise. Bishops also protect church members' rights. By carrying out these varied duties, bishops ensure the church stays true to its gospel mission and serves the needs of its people in each new generation. Their role is essential for a church wishing to maintain continuity with its historical foundations.

THE CHIEF PASTOR

One of the best ways to describe the office and role of the bishop is with a metaphor from the shepherd's world: Pastor. The bishop is the chief pastor and is responsible for the spiritual care and guidance of the faithful under his jurisdiction. He provides counseling, prayer, and teaching to nurture members' faith. Through preaching and theological discussion, the bishop explains and spreads the doctrines and beliefs of the church. His sacramental ministry involves overseeing the administration of rites like the Eucharist, which is central to the Christian life.

The bishop also leads the church community as a shepherd tends to his flock. He is tasked with supporting, addressing conflicts, and guiding the faithful through difficulties. Overseeing the work of local clergy is another critical duty: the bishop ensures priests and deacons fulfill their roles properly and adhere to church teachings. He may have to intervene if problems arise.

Administratively, the bishop manages diocesan affairs, including finances. He strives to use resources efficiently to meet community needs. In all aspects of leadership, the bishop aims to care for the faithful and proclaim the gospel just as Christ commissioned. His broad pastoral role is essential to nurturing a strong church. Through his diverse responsibilities, the bishop lives out a calling to serve God and God's people.

CHIEF TEACHER AND PROPAGATOR

As chief teacher, the bishop is responsible for proclaiming and explaining the doctrines and traditions of the faith. He elucidates the Bible and church teachings through preaching, writing, and public discussion, making them relevant to current issues. He also safeguards tradition, ensuring the faithful transmission of beliefs across generations.

In addition, the bishop propagates the faith by promoting Gospel values in the public sphere and engaging other religions in dialogue. He prepares future church leaders by recruiting and rigorously screening seminary candidates. The bishop oversees religious education programs to nurture the spiritual growth of the faithful. His multifaceted teaching role is vital for passing on the rich theological heritage and applying it to emerging challenges.

. . .

An Agent of Unity

The bishop serves as the primary agent of unity within the church and diocese. He promotes communion by building relationships between clergy, laity, and parishes to foster a shared sense of mission. When conflicts arise, the bishop acts as a mediator to bring about reconciliation and understanding between opposing parties. He may make a final ruling to resolve a dispute in limited cases.

To maintain orthodoxy, the bishop addresses false doctrines and upholds sound church teachings. This protects the integrity of the faith and enables the church to unite around shared beliefs. Through policies and programs, the bishop establishes guidelines for cooperation between parishes and collaboration in pastoral services.

The bishop also regularly visits parishes to develop personal connections with the faithful. This allows him to better attend to needs and provide support across the diocese. By fulfilling these diverse duties, the bishop nurtures an environment of unity so the church can effectively live out its Gospel mission worldwide. His leadership as an agent of unity is critical for a church seeking harmony amidst diversity.

After a five-point description of the roles assigned to the bishop, we should all begin to pray for our bishops. The role of the bishop is an enormous burden for those who are called and consecrated to the office. The bishop is a visible sign of the church, a defender of the faith, a chief pastor, a chief teacher, and an agent of unity. It is an extraordinary role with incredible responsibilities, opportunities, challenges, and potential.

The bishop should be a symbol of unity and a promoter of peace. He should be a bridge of love, a mediator for concord, and an instrument of communion. Let him be patient, kind, and gentle; let him always listen and forgive. Let him be unwavering in his faith, firm in his hope, and steadfast with charity.

— SAINT CYPRIAN, LETTER 67

Bishops know their roles and responsibilities. But most of us can see the enormous challenge they face. If we list the various metaphors and roles that a bishop is called to embody, we can see an obvious challenge. Some of the images/metaphors appear to be mutually exclusive. Can one be a "shepherd" and a "defender" simultaneously? It is hard to comfort and correct someone at the same time. Both aspects may be needed, but it is a difficult task.

And when things start to go sideways for a clergy member or a congregation of the bishop, how can he effectively pastor, correct, discipline, and comfort? All at once? He must, to be sure. Clergy and congregations need to be kept in line, so to speak. It is *aligned* with the faith once delivered to the saints (Jude 1:3). So how can the bishop do this vital work?

AWKWARD TRIANGLES

Strong, healthy relationships between a bishop, rector, and congregation are essential for the church's flourishing. However, the dynamics between these three can sometimes lead to a harmful occurrence known as triangulation. This happens when conflict or discomfort leads one party to involve a third party rather than dealing directly with the other. Bishops and rectors should follow certain guidelines to avoid triangulation and nurture productive relationships.

- The bishop should resist getting overly involved unless there are serious issues. Generally, trust the rector's leadership.
- If congregants complain to the bishop about the rector, the bishop should redirect them to speak directly to the rector first, then follow up with the rector if needed. Avoid reacting to one side.
- The rector should have the bishop's support in leading the congregation. If issues arise, the rector should speak directly to the bishop before involving others.
- Vestry members should have clear roles and responsibilities. The rector leads them in managing affairs. The bishop does not micromanage vestry business.
- Transparency in decision-making processes helps avoid secrecy that breeds triangulation. Keep appropriate people informed through proper channels.
- Periodic combined meetings of the bishop, rector, and vestry build connections and understanding. Pray for one another.

The goal is direct, open communication between all parties, with the bishop supporting and guiding the rector, who leads the vestry in a healthy manner for the congregation's good. Avoiding triangulation dynamics will allow for better relationships.

Another illustration might help us see how the bishop can perform his duties with love and grace, avoiding triangulation and supporting and guiding rectors and congregations.

TO ILLUSTRATE: THE SEVEN TOOLS IN THE BISHOP'S TOOLBOX

Occasionally, I will attend a woodworking class at a unique early American heritage organization a few hours away. The artisans and craftsmen there are highly skilled in creating fine furniture. I attend these classes because they have a simple philosophy of craftsmanship. No power tools. They make furniture with only hand tools, as craftsmen did in the mid-1800s. I love it.

This craftsman community believes and teaches woodworkers that any piece of furniture can be made by hand using seven tools. A woodworking shop should have only a few implements to use—but they should be the proper implements. And they should be sharp. The hand plane, the saw, the chisel, a mallet, a square, a marking tool, and a tape measure. With just those tools, a woodworker can build anything. Believe it or not, it is true. With practiced skill, sharp tools, and a steady hand, a craftsman can make any piece of furniture.

When I read through the Constitutions and Canons of the ACNA and the historic and biblical roles and responsibilities of a diocesan bishop, I think that rectors, vestries, and bishops should know that the bishop also has tools to use in the service of his office. They are not power tools. There are no fast solutions to most problems and challenges we face in the church. Most of the tools that the bishop has available to him are old-fashioned. But most of them are remarkably effective.

Consider what the bishop can do to guard and defend the church's doctrine, disciplines, and worship in his diocese. He has seven tools. The first five are preventative; the last two are corrective.

FIVE PREVENTATIVE TOOLS IN THE BISHOP'S TOOLBOX

1. **The Annual Visitation:** The canons require the bishop to visit his congregation regularly. This visit should not be perfunctory. There should be opportunities for the bishop to contact the rector and family.

2. **The Constitution and Canons:** Admittedly, they do not make stirring reading, but all should know the rules we use to govern ourselves. The C&C shows our members, clergy, and leaders that discipline, decisions, and actions that are warranted are not arbitrary.

3. **Training and Deployment:** Each diocese has different ways to train, call, hire, and deploy deacons and priests. Early in any training process, the bishop can determine which person has the right temperament and character traits to serve in the church.

4. **The Clericus:** Each bishop can call his deacons and priests together for in-service training and biblical teaching. Most clergy consider these retreats and conferences time for needed fellowship, encouragement, problem-sharing, solving, and worship. They are often greatly needed and provide perspective and personal renewal.

5. **The Discretionary Fund:** Bishops need access to enough money to provide their clergy with financial assistance when needed. The bishop can help provide for marital counseling, summer camp subsidies for children of clergy, assistance to attend required conferences, or a myriad of other ways to help strengthen the morale and stamina of the church leaders.

TWO CORRECTIVE TOOLS IN THE BISHOP'S TOOLBOX

The final two actions or tools available to the bishop may seem harsh or heavy-handed. But there are times when clear action and direction are needed. The Canon provides for the use of these tools under Title IV.

1. **The Godly Admonition:** Sometimes, a bishop must step into a messy situation and solve a festering problem or a pastoral crisis. A godly admonition is a directive from the diocesan bishop to a priest or deacon about a specific situation for which guidance is needed. The bishop writes this directive only after meeting with the clergy personally. The admonition is specific and actionable, and it must be obeyed.

2. **The Written Inhibition:** Inhibition is a temporary suspension of a priest or deacon from ministry, in whole or in part. The bishop can issue an inhibition if he believes the priest or deacon has engaged in conduct unbecoming a member of the clergy. An inhibition is rendered with the advice and consent of the diocesan standing committee or other elected leadership team.

As you can see, there are several tools that the bishop has in his toolbox. Some are *preventative*. They help foster a strong pastoral connection between the bishop, priest, or deacon. Some are *protective*. They can keep erroneous teaching and teachers from leading people astray. Some tools are *pastoral*. They allow the bishop to care for the clergy and families in the diocese. And some of these tools are *corrective*. They stop offending or misguided clergy from further damaging themselves, their church, or others.

Tools such as these are helpful for the bishop's role and responsibilities in the diocese. They can help the bishop create and maintain a culture of fellowship, trust, and confidence. As the bishop works in his diocese, he should always consider how best to serve the cause of Christ by serving the clergy and the people of the diocese.

THE COLOR PURPLE

As we close these chapters on the role and office of the bishop, we should remember why the ecclesiastical color of a bishop's office is purple. The bishop is often dressed in a purple shirt, wears an amethyst ring, and dons purple robes. Years ago, my bishop sometimes signed his letters using a purple ink pen! But why?

The Book of Acts describes how Peter, the first bishop, preached the first Christian sermon on the Day of Pentecost. The sermon explained the miraculous events when the Holy Spirit came upon Jesus's disciples. Some people in the crowd wrongly thought the disciples were drunk, even though it was only 9 AM. Peter refuted this accusation by saying the disciples were not drunk but filled with the Holy Spirit. To make this point, he used the Greek word "amethystos," which meant "not intoxicated." This is the origin of the word "amethyst" we use today.

The color purple reminds bishops of the calling to preach the Gospel as Peter did in Jerusalem at Pentecost. It is a reminder that they are not to be drunk on wine but instead on the power of the Holy Spirit.

So be it!

---

1. From the Chicago-Lambeth Quadrilateral, 1888 statement on Anglican identity.

RECAP: LOOKING BACK ON
THE LEADERSHIP ROLES

The rector serves as a congregation's spiritual leader and visionary, responsible for casting vision, building ministry teams, providing spiritual leadership, maintaining accountability, and developing stewardship. As Chief Visionary Officer, the rector clearly articulates where the church is headed, reflects on its history, determines needed resources, and builds a collaborative team for the journey. With pastoral authority, the rector oversees worship, discipleship, outreach, and communication to foster congregational health. Maintaining spiritual vitality and work-life balance is essential.

The vestry supports the rector through sound administrative governance and counsel. Rather than manage programs, they protect the systems enabling ministry by upholding the church's vision and plans, ensuring financial integrity through oversight and modeling generosity, advocating for the rector, and planning for pastoral succession. Wardens provide wisdom and accountability alongside the rector. Serving in these capacities allows the vestry to act as stewards of the church with faithfulness and skill.

The bishop represents apostolic succession, providing spiritual authority and accountability to defend doctrine and nurture missional unity. Consecrated as pastor, teacher, and shepherd for the diocese, he bears profound influence through oversight of clergy, liturgy, teaching, and pastoral presence. A grandfatherly approach of occasional counsel and relationship best facilitates subsidiarity. Diocesan health requires the bishop to remain rooted in prayer and model humility, service, and Christlike care.

In the Anglican system, clarity surrounding the interdependent roles of rector, vestry, and bishop is vital for congregational flourishing. The rector gives innovative and steady leadership, the vestry governs with wisdom, and the bishop protects unity with truth and grace.

Each plays a leadership role and shares in the responsibility for fulfilling the church's apostolic calling.

AFTERWORD

The Anglican Church in North America has been blessed
with devoted leaders united by their love for Jesus Christ
and commitment to proclaiming the Gospel. As this
book has illustrated, the rector, vestry, and bishop each play vital
roles in leading local congregations. While their backgrounds may
vary, their dedication does not.

Rectors serve as chief visionary leaders, guiding their churches with
passion and purpose. Vestries provide invaluable support through
their spiritual leadership and governance. Bishops oversee the
health of congregations, connecting them to the broader diocesan
family. Despite differences in worship style or emphasis, the
unifying power of Christ enables these leaders to work together for
His glory.

I hope this book has clarified the distinct yet complementary roles
of rectors, vestries, and bishops. With sound understanding comes
more effective unity. I pray that this resource has equipped both
new and experienced leaders to lead Anglican churches with focus
and alignment.

There is important work ahead as we seek to grow God's kingdom. But when rectors, vestries, and bishops embrace their unique callings, the possibilities are endless. We serve an infinitely powerful God who does more than we can imagine. May we rely on His strength alone as we write the unfolding story of the Anglican Church in North America for generations to come.

———

THE PURPOSE OF THIS BOOK HAS BEEN TO LAY OUT, as best I can, the vital relationship between the rector, the vestry, and the bishop. The connection and support between the three are critical for any ministry or mission to succeed.

LeaderWorks is the non-profit ministry I began in 2016 when I left the parish of Christ Church. My purpose is to help leaders do their work; to that end, I hope this book will be helpful.

If I may be of help to you and your organization, please do not hesitate to contact me at David@LeaderWorks.org.

APPENDIX

Some of the material in the Appendix will not impact every church; perhaps it will be useful to only a few. But it is included in order to help every church at any age or stage.

APPENDIX

APPENDIX A: MISCELLANEOUS IMPORTANT THINGS

A DOZEN POINTS THAT NEED TO BE MADE AND REMEMBERED

My wife and I have a drawer in the kitchen filled with cabinets and drawers for cooking utensils, pots, pans, plates, glasses, flatware, and assorted dishes. Each of the drawers has a particular purpose. We try to stay organized that way, as do most families, so that we can find things when we need them.

But we also have what we call a Junk Drawer. And in speaking to other people about their own kitchen, I think that almost everyone has a catch-all drawer like that. It doesn't mean that the items in the drawer are junk. It means that if you can remember what is in the drawer, you know exactly where to find them!

IMPORTANT THINGS IN THAT JUNK DRAWER

With that in mind, here is the chapter dedicated to the things that should be remembered but don't easily fit any other place in the book. They may have been glossed over. But here is a random list of what the vestry and rector need to know or to do. These ideas and items are part of the unique Anglican polity I outlined earlier in the book.

1. The members of a congregation do not vote on anything except who is elected to the vestry. The vestry votes on everything else. For example, the annual budget is never subject to a vote from the members of the congregation. In the language of *Robert's Rules of Order*, the vestry does not "move" the budget for approval by the congregation. The budget is presented to the congregation for their information as a completed item of business.

2. A rector is not a member of the church they lead. This was mentioned early in the book, but it would be easy to overlook. The rector and other clergy are not members of the congregation. They are members of the diocese.

3. The entire staff, ordained or lay, report to and serve at the pleasure of the rector. The rector can hire and fire staff members without the permission of the vestry, much less the bishop. A trusted rector will never take precipitous action, however. Usually, any staff dismissals are the subject of serious discussion and prayer at a vestry meeting. However, the rector does not need permission to exercise this authority.

4. The vestry does not have the authority to hire or fire the rector. Once installed, the rector has tenure in the position and cannot be terminated by the vestry. This differs from secular boards that hire and oversee a CEO. If ongoing conflicts arise between the rector and vestry members, the diocese's canons outline a process for resolution that involves consulting the bishop. Vestries should familiarize themselves with these canons for guidance should such a situation occur.

5. The bishop and the rectors of all congregations in a diocese are the only clergy with tenure. That is, they have

permanent roles. In the case of the rector of a church, his tenure is granted to him by the bishop at the installation service. Remember, he isn't a member of the parish and doesn't work for the church or the vestry.

6. In the case of the rector's absence, resignation, death, or termination through appropriate channels, the "next in charge" of the congregation is not the Assistant or Associate Rector. It is the senior warden! A layperson representing the entire vestry is placed in the leadership role. Proactive and wise senior wardens will immediately call for prayer and ask the bishop to help appoint an Interim or Priest-in-Charge while a formal search process is conducted.

7. Both a church and a non-profit are tax-exempt organizations registered as a 501(c)3 entity. But a church is not a non-profit organization in the same way that a non-profit charity is. They are very different entities and need to be considered as distinct. Consider their funding and development. Most churches have donors who are the primary recipients of the church's ministry; most donors to non-profits are not the target audience for the non-profit. Churches foster personal relationships among donors and between the rector and donors; donors for charities and non-profits seldom meet. Churches typically have larger donors and fewer of them than local charities; non-profits seek to have a vast donor base that gives relatively smaller gifts. This is why participating in a non-profit donation drive, like Giving Tuesday, is inappropriate for the local church.

8. People who serve on a vestry are typically not chosen because they have unique gifts and abilities needed in the church. There are exceptions to this, but they are few. An unexpected resignation from the vestry can often allow the vestry to ask, "What kind of person do we need to

serve with us?" The senior warden or the rector can recruit the specific person to be elected to fulfill the unexpired term of the resigned member.

9. The larger the church, the fewer ways it feels connected to the diocese. The smaller the church, the more it relies upon the programs and resources a diocese can provide. Consequently, the larger the church, the less it uses the programs and resources that may be available through the diocese.

10. I mentioned earlier that a rector should never surprise a vestry with a brand-new idea or a quick and sudden turn. This is practical wisdom from years of leading vestry meetings. If it is unwise to surprise a vestry with new ideas that need immediate action, it is nearly a sin to surprise a senior warden at a vestry meeting!

11. The doctrine and beliefs of the Anglican Church in North America are stated in the Preamble to its Constitution and Canons. They cannot be changed, altered, or modified except by the decisions of the College of Bishops over two successive Provincial Assemblies. In other words, the eight points of the Preamble are in a "lockbox" and cannot be changed.

12. The College of Bishops takes their duty to guard the church's faith, unity, and discipline as a solemn oath. They cannot be lobbied or pressured into certain actions or changes by any forces inside or outside the church.

APPENDIX B: TEN CRITICAL AREAS FOR VESTRY OVERSIGHT

DO NOT NEGLECT THESE ESSENTIAL THINGS

Oversight is a challenging function to achieve. On the one hand, the overseers can seem to be too nosy or meddlesome in the course of their oversight. On the other hand, a church has a vestry to ensure that certain things are overseen. Here are ten areas in which the vestry must have some oversight. It does not have to be daily or even monthly, but both the rector and the vestry will want to be sure that these areas are responsibly cared for.

1. DISCRETIONARY FUNDS

It is normal for a rector to have funds that can be used at their discretion. By nature, these gifts are intended to be discreet and given under the exclusive control of the rector. The rector is often in a closer and more pastoral relationship with the parish's people, allowing them to see the actual human needs. For example, a rector may know a seminarian who needs financial support. The rector can decide to donate to a mission fund or a worthy faith-based project that supports or amplifies the church's vision.

Typically, the needs that a discretionary fund is set up to meet are, as mentioned, discreet. These needs are, by nature, unbudgeted or underfunded. Sometimes, they are brought to the attention of the rector suddenly. A vestry should set up a rector's discretionary fund at the bank. It should be communicated to the parish members that this benevolence fund exists so that they can make donations to it, and the rectors should be able to direct the use of this fund without general vestry awareness.

However, you can immediately see the challenge that this might pose for the IRS or an auditor. If the rector has unbridled use over these funds, and they are entirely hidden from the oversight of the vestry, there will be many opportunities for misuse. If these funds are misused intentionally or innocently, this can short-circuit the level of trust in a congregation.

In my experience, the best safeguards for this kind of fund are as follows:

- A bookkeeper should keep records of the income and expenses for this fund. In other words, no separate, hidden checking account or checkbook should exist. This fund should be part of the church's restricted accounts.
- Members of the church can and should be invited to give to this fund in addition to their regular contributions.
- It is possible that a person would want to give money to the rector's discretionary fund instead of the church's operating fund. This should be noted for the treasurer to see and account for in the financial records.
- The rector should note the purpose of the expenditure on every check, and the bookkeeper can retrieve that description.
- Generally speaking, donors should not assume they can direct the use of the money they give to the rector's discretionary fund.

- No funds from this account should ever be provided directly to the rector or any family member.
- The rector should ask the senior warden to review all expenditures annually. If two or three payments are made for a regular or recurring need, the warden should recommend that the church's annual budget cover these expenses.

In the past, the IRS has had some heartburn over the rector's discretionary fund issue, and some dioceses and bishops strongly discourage it. The local vestry should be sure they know the challenges of a discretionary fund and provide the proper safeguards. In some dioceses, the bishop forbids the church to have a discretionary fund. Local experience, history, and customs should be considered.

Once again, it is always a good idea to ask someone on the vestry or the finance team to review the use of these funds on an annual basis. While the use of the funds may be discreet, they are not to be confidential.

2. RESTRICTED AND DESIGNATED FUNDS

In general, only two kinds of funds come into a church. First, unrestricted funds are freely given for the operating fund of the parish to pay salaries, bills, expenses, fund programs, and support the church's day-to-day operations. The second kind of fund is a restricted fund. Some churches have many restricted funds but are treated the same way.

In other words, there are only two kinds of funds: unrestricted funds to operate and support the church and everything else. There may be a building fund, a flower fund, a vacation Bible school fund, or a mission fund. But they are all the same kind of fund: restricted for use as designated by the vestry.

Restricted funds involve gifts to the church where either the donor(s) or the vestry restricts how the funds or assets may be spent or used. For example, if a donor restricts how a donation is used, the church has a legal, ethical, and moral obligation to use it as intended. If the church wants to use them for something else or in a slightly different manner, they must talk with the donor to be clear and above reproach. There may be times when the church designates funds for a specific purpose. For example, they decide that the offering at a special service (like Ash Wednesday) will be given to a local ministry partner. These things should be documented appropriately in the vestry minutes and subject to the proper financial protocols.

It is not uncommon for older churches to have a plethora of unspent restricted funds in the bank. Again, they are all the same kind of money: restricted. Believe it or not, some vestries are paralyzed as to what to do with some of these funds. Perhaps the need for the funds' use has long since passed. The school that was being supported has closed its doors. The mission trip is over, and funds collected and unused are sitting in the church's accounts.

This is not a serious problem for most vestries, but funds should be used, redirected, or returned to the donor. Here are a few bits of wisdom I have picked up over the years.

The vestry can develop a simple policy to have a sunset on all restricted funds after five years. After a specific time, the vestry can reallocate restricted funds to a new purpose. This doesn't need to be trumpeted, but a standing policy will be a helpful tool.

The vestry can always refuse a donation. For example, the vestry can refuse or return the gift if a donor gives a significant gift to a pet cause or project not part of the church's mission.

Usually, a pastoral conversation between the rector and the donor or the donor's family can free up a fund with stated but undesired restrictions.

Some vestries like these unspent funds in their accounts for obvious reasons. It is a buffer or a cushion against a low balance in the operating fund. It is accurate, and while the funds in the restricted fund (of any variety) should not be permanently transferred to the operating fund, they can be borrowed during lean times. However, the presence of any large balances in the restricted fund can create some unintended consequences. First, they can create a false positive about the actual financial condition of the church. The vestry and church members might feel fortified by having a lot of money "on the side" and, therefore, might miss the warning signs of a church in stewardship trouble.

There is at least one other reason why a high fund balance in the restricted fund might have negative ramifications. The vestry should remember that people give to a church for the congregation to use in the service of its mission. Funds are not supposed to be kept, hoarded, or stockpiled. Every church needs a prudential reserve, but they do not need to be sitting on a lot of money. As donors see the fattened condition of the church's financial picture, they will give their money to another ministry or church.

3. PRUDENTIAL RESERVE

Regarding financial savings, a church vestry will always need a full, prayerful, and honest conversation about the money it keeps in its coffers and the money it spends for its mission and ministry.

Imagine your church receives a financial windfall. For some, this would be a significant blessing. But for other churches, such a "blessing" could put them out of business. Why? Because they would not know what to do with that asset. Their members might cross their arms with satisfaction and thus close their wallets. People who had supported the church for years might feel their money was no longer needed. The vestry, now feeling flush with cash, might hire more staff than they need, which would, in turn, turn off the volunteer strength of the church. It doesn't take too much imagination to think of how a massive windfall of money could cause a downward spiral in life and vitality.

Yet, the church vestry should be wise about saving money and holding some funds in a reserve account for future use or plans. We all should do that in our own lives. It is challenging for a financially stretched church to imagine a time when they would have the luxury of putting money away for a "rainy day."

There is another approach that some people on a vestry will promote. This is a "faith-budget" approach. It sounds like it should be the right thing for a church to advocate. Indeed, a church should walk and budget by faith. In fact, from a certain point of view, every dollar given and spent in a church is given in faith. But a "faith-budget" approach would have only a little money for savings. After all, God pays for what he orders, it is said. But there is ample evidence in Scripture about the need for savings plans, insurance, retirement funding, and the wise use of money. Setting aside a certain amount of money as a reserve does not indicate a lack of faith or a deeper faith. Saving cash is a good business practice that a church can and should employ.

BUT HOW MUCH?

In determining an amount that the church should have set aside in savings, consider these important facts:

- The church is the only non-profit that gathers its donor base once a week. If the church ever gets into immediate danger or crisis, a congregational meeting with its donor base is at most six days away.

- Everyone in your church wants your church to thrive.
- Communications about the financial needs of a congregation are quickly drawn up and disseminated.
- Most financial crises are quickly addressed, at least initially, by asking people to give.

So, how much should the church have in savings? The church should have 3–4 months of operating cash as a buffer. Once in place, the church would not need to worry about low times or a snowstorm when services might need to be canceled. I do not imagine that any donors would balk at that amount being held in reserve. Many donors would rest assured that their church is acting wisely.

This amount might seem an easy achievement for some churches. The younger and smaller churches might never imagine having that kind of security. But every church must address this aspect of financial planning and preparation. In concert with the rector, the vestry will need to know when to save these funds and, once saved, when to spend them.

4. RECTOR'S COMPENSATION

The role of the vestry is to provide financial support to the rector. This is an essential role and certainly cannot fall to the rector to decide. Your diocese might have a recommended minimum standard that you can reference, but from my experience, it probably needs to be higher. The vestry should not expect the rector to "make a bid" for their salary. That puts the spiritual leader in the unwanted role of a negotiator.

There are nine areas of financial compensation that the vestry should consider. Most of them will be set for the vestry by costs and rates of, for example, health care. Once these costs are established and fixed into an annual budget, the rest of the compensation can be adjusted according to sound wisdom and financial stewardship.

The nine areas for consideration are these:

- Salary costs for a full-time Rector
- Housing allowance
- Social Security reimbursement
- Health insurance, vision, dental, etc.
- Retirement funding
- Automobile allowance
- Continuing education
- Hospitality and Ministry expenses
- Travel allowance

Young churches without a history of clergy compensation might struggle to meet these expenses and be forced to choose which to fund and which to delay, which may be a last resort for the vestry. It is often true that clergy are more than willing to forgo and carry these expenses personally.

The vestry would be wise to pray about these issues, receive guidance from other vestries and congregational leaders, and explain these costs to the parish winsomely. Most churches want to be as generous as possible with their rectors.

One part of the clergy compensation is unique to all clergy and often needs a further explanation for vestry members. Currently, in the United States of America, a special law provision allows clergy to exclude their housing allowance from reportable income, provided that the vestry designates explicitly a portion of their salary for that purpose. As part of the annual budget process, the vestry should review and approve housing allowances for applicable clergy each year. Even if housing is provided, there may be a general maintenance and upkeep allowance. This should be reflected in the minutes.

The vestry is responsible for designating the amount before the tax year in which it is claimed. In other words, it is not retroactive. You will find a lot of information on the internet about the Clergy Housing Allowance provision.

While it is a definite financial gain for the minister, it should be remembered that the amount excluded from income taxes has no impact on the church budget; it is just a category of compensation.

Awkward Moment

The subject and discussion of money may cause an awkward moment for the rector and the vestry, but it is essential to have it. Very important. No minister is working in the church to get rich. None of us do this for money. But if a vestry is unwilling to talk about their Rector's compensation and do the right thing, it sends a very discouraging message to the Rector.

To ease the awkwardness of the conversation, I suggest this pattern of discussion:

In the Fall, the senior warden and rector should discuss compensation. The rector is asked to pray about the needs of their family and the level of compensation they receive, keeping in mind the financial strength and age of the congregation. The rector might take the occasion to speak with a financial planner to assess the family's financial health.

The rector and senior warden should have a follow-up meeting before the vestry ratifies the annual budget.

The vestry and rector can meet to discuss the budget, the allocation of funds, the vision for the year ahead, and some of the goals and efforts that will be set.

The vestry can go into "Executive Session" and ask the rector to leave the meeting. The senior warden can relate past conversations with the rector and suggest adjustments to their compensation.

But How Much?

This is a complex subject because every church's ability to fund a rector position will differ. Some rectors are bi-vocational or work as church volunteers and gain their living through outside employment. Some rectors are retired and have an income apart from the church budget. Some rectors need the church to be much more generous with their compensation package because of personal needs. As I say, it is difficult to give guidance on this. Some reports and worksheets that address the Sr. Pastor's compensation are available online. Often, a diocese might have a suggested minimum standard that should be met. In some situations, these standards might be helpful; they are usually not.

I have suggested a unique way of benchmarking compensation levels in the church for the rector and any staff. I honestly cannot remember where I first heard this plan, but it can be beneficial in getting into the ballpark regarding compensation for the rector. The local school system has published salaries and benefits packages for teachers and administrators. There are similar categories between the two disciplines of education and ministry. I am not equating the work of one with the work of another, but public school pay scales can be a helpful benchmark for vestry members to consider, adjusted as needed.

Here are some additional thoughts on compensation for clergy:

- Clergy compensation should be competitive with other professions in the community.
- Clergy compensation should be fair and equitable, considering the congregation's size and financial resources.

- Clergy compensation should be based on the qualifications and experience of the individual.
- Clergy compensation should be reviewed and adjusted regularly to remain competitive and fair.

It is important to remember that clergy compensation is not just about money. It is also about recognizing the value of the work that clergy do. Clergy are called to serve God and their congregations. They provide spiritual leadership, pastoral care, and education. They work long hours and often have to make sacrifices. They deserve to be compensated fairly for their work.

5. FACILITIES

The issue of facilities is very complex within the ACNA. Some parishes have historic buildings and properties. Some have lost their buildings and are in the process of creating new spaces. Many of our church plants rent facilities and will be involved in building projects soon. The vestry does not need to serve as the project manager or real estate agent but must know what is happening in this area. They need to know the costs for capital improvements, operational costs, and maintenance needs. They should budget accordingly for them. They must also make sure they are following local regulations in terms of their facilities and facility usage. One key thing is to set a clear policy about usage. Are buildings and facilities available for rental and use by outside groups? What protocols govern this process? Facilities should be safe, clean, and legally compliant for each congregation. Further regulations for a columbarium or cemetery on the church grounds will exist. Historical properties will also have their own issues with local compliance and regulation.

Vestries should receive counsel and wisdom from bankers, realtors, and other professionals when renting, leasing, purchasing, or renovating any facility. It is beyond the scope of this book to give advice or direction other than to say that your vestry should seek sound advice and guidance.

6. INSURANCE

The church needs to carry appropriate and reasonable levels of insurance. The vestry should make sure that this is done. If the church owns property, there should be appropriate levels of property insurance. There should also be insurance and a proper inventory of church assets. The church should carry general liability insurance, insurance for any motor vehicles, and directors' and officers' liability insurance. In addition, there will be workers' compensation insurance, health insurance for clergy and staff, and disability insurance. I recommend that each church work with an insurance agent who can create a complete policy to cover their needs. The vestry will ensure this happens and generally work on proper risk management.

7. CHILD AND MEMBER PROTECTION

A church is a wonderful family of faith that strives to welcome all people without judgment. However, in our eagerness to grow our congregations and fill volunteer positions, churches can sometimes fail to vet the people who offer to serve. While we aim to be warm and accepting communities, sadly, this welcoming nature can attract individuals looking to take advantage of the trust placed in them.

Thus, safeguarding our most vulnerable members - especially children and youth - must be a top priority. The vestry has a solemn duty to implement rigorous background checks, abuse prevention training, and other protective measures to shield young parishioners from potential harm. We must thoroughly screen all new volunteers, employees, and clergy. Even when a pastor comes to us ordained and with glowing recommendations, we must ensure the diocese has fully vetted them carefully before granting them authority in our parish.

Recently, we have become increasingly aware that dangers can also come from within. Spiritual abuse, sexual misconduct, and toxic church cultures can flourish when left unchecked, potentially inflicting lasting damage on adults in our congregations. As leaders, we must be vigilant to prevent such abuses of power and breaches of trust. We must hold ourselves and our fellow church officers to the highest ethical standards, with humility and accountability before God.

By taking every precaution to guard against predators and enacting policies that protect the vulnerable, we hope to make our church a true sanctuary. Our goal is physical safety and the emotional, spiritual, and psychological well-being of all who join our faith community. With God's help, we can become a church where all are embraced in His love as we nurture one another in grace.

The vestry must be diligent and unwavering in its pursuit of a church that is both safe and welcoming for all. We cannot sacrifice one for the other. With prayer, discernment, and the guidance of the Holy Spirit, we can create an atmosphere of trust, accountability, and care that allows everyone to flourish.

8. BY-LAWS AND POLICIES

This is the boring part of the role of the vestry...until it isn't. If a congregation gets to a point where it is referring to policies and by-laws to prove a point or bolster an argument, it is not usually a good thing. The vestry should have an ongoing duty to regularly establish, evaluate, and formally review all by-laws and operational policies. Again, it is not exciting work and should usually occur apart from the vestry's monthly meeting. For example, what is the policy for the use of the building? If the church does not have a clear statement of who can and cannot rent or use the property or facilities, it could be a problem. If one group is allowed to use the building without charge (like a Boy Scout troop) and another group asks to borrow the facility, what is the policy for usage? If the second group wants to hold a meeting that violates the closely held faith beliefs of the church, how can a church say no?

Some by-laws could be written proscribing or allowing building use, for example. By-laws might usually guide the process of searching for a new rector. By-laws might establish the Annual Meeting's date, time, and length to allow flexibility. Most by-laws should allow for the vestry to vote electronically via email. The point is that if there is no policy, the church can continue for years and then suddenly be greeted by a problem for which there is no written practice or the written by-law is outdated.

As I mentioned, creating and maintaining good, clear policies and by-laws is not exciting work. They may never be acutely needed, but it is good to have them handy and ready when they are.

9. LEGAL ISSUES AND OPINIONS

Having a lawyer who volunteers their time or offers their services at a discount to the parish is always a good idea. There are legal issues that the vestry needs to be aware of as they work with the rector as he leads the vision. For example, it might be that the rector and staff need to have an upgraded copier for the church. That is usually a lease agreement, and the vestry must be comfortable that the church is not entering into the wrong or wrongheaded contract. There are personnel issues that a church is constantly dealing with. In dismissing a key staff person, will the church be subject to legal action for wrongful termination? If the church purchases a piece of land, a lawyer will be needed to review the documents. This legal function is a vital role for some attorneys to assume. The traditional name for this role is "Chancellor," They often add significant value to vestry discussions. A chancellor can often be consulted in real-time if they attend a vestry meeting. They have a voice but no vote in all matters.

10. BANKING, BANKS, AND CREDIT

Finally, a church needs a positive and factual relationship with a local bank. There are many transactions that a church engages in over a month. The number cannot be known, but I guess it is larger than the average client or customer of the local bank. Consider all the EFT transactions, checks, auto-drafts, and bill payments that come in and out of the local church on a routine basis. In addition, as mentioned above, a congregation can have a good-sized balance in a savings account or a rainy-day fund (unless it is raining!). All of this is music to the ears of a bank. It is always a good practice for the rector and the local banker to be on a first-name basis.

In addition, I often counsel churches to establish a line of credit for emergencies. The best time to take out a line of credit, as most bankers and all lawyers will attest, is when you don't need one. It is just a precaution so that the vestry and the parish can act freely to seize unique opportunities as they present themselves.

APPENDIX C: THE SEARCH PROCESS OVERVIEW

BEST PRACTICES FOR THE (HOPEFULLY) OCCASIONAL NEED TO SEARCH FOR A NEW RECTOR

Before you read what I say about the Search Process, I invite you to visit the Diocese of Western Anglicans website. Bishop Keith Andrews is a friend of mine, and he and his team have developed some outstanding resources. He told me the diocese would love to share them with the broader ACNA. They are worth reading and adapting to your situation. The web address is in the Bibliography.

When embarking on the search process to find the next Rector, the vestry should address three key questions. It is crucial to answer these questions upfront and communicate the answers to the rest of the congregation.

- What is the bishop's role in selecting the new rector? It is important to clarify this, as the bishop's involvement varies among dioceses. Some bishops prefer to receive a list of finalists for vetting, while others take a more hands-off approach. The vestry should understand and communicate the bishop's role to the congregation.

- What role does the congregation play in choosing the next rector? While the congregation does not have a vote in the selection process, keeping them informed about the process the vestry intends to follow is vital. Regular updates should be provided, and on the day of the announcement, the decision should be communicated, and the candidate introduced either in person or through a video.

- Who makes the final decision? Although the vestry ultimately makes the final decision, it should be made clear to the Search Committee that the vestry desires multiple candidates for consideration. This ensures a thorough evaluation of options before reaching a decision.

By addressing these questions upfront and effectively communicating the process to the congregation, the vestry can ensure transparency in the search for the next rector. This fosters confidence in the selection process and facilitates a smoother transition to the new rector.

Here are ten things a vestry should do or be aware of during the search process for a new rector:

1. Seek assistance and resources from the bishop and diocesan office, establishing a timeline, prayer support team, and communication strategy to inform the congregation.
2. Consider forming a dedicated search committee comprising key leaders from the congregation or engage a consultant or retired rector to guide the process.

3. Compile essential information about the parish's state and vision and request the outgoing rector to draft the position description before departure.

4. Prepare a comprehensive parish profile based on the gathered information and advertise the open position through various channels.

5. Determine the compensation range early on in consultation with the parish's finance team.

6. Review resumes with patience and prayerfulness, narrowing down candidates for further conversations, reference checks, and visits.

7. Exhibit patience, prayerfulness, and wisdom throughout the search process, ensuring the church's vision and values are not solely reliant on the outgoing or incoming rector.

8. Foster flexibility and openness upon the new rector's arrival, eagerly anticipating the new things God will do among them during the next phase of congregational life.

9. Avoid hasty decisions, premature judgments, or losing focus on the ongoing mission and ministry of the church. Maintain a steady and discerning approach, balancing urgency with patience.

10. Establish a detailed process for selecting a new rector in advance, either by incorporating it into the parish's by-laws or keeping it as a policy to be implemented when needed.

A SUCCESSFUL SEARCH PROCESS FOR A NEW RECTOR necessitates careful planning, discernment, and collaboration among the vestry, search committee, bishop, and diocesan officials. By following these guidelines, seeking assistance when necessary, and utilizing available resources, the vestry can ensure that the new rector possesses the leadership qualities required to enable the congregation to thrive and fulfill its mission and ministry.

Throughout this guidebook, we have emphasized the significance of healthy leadership for vibrant churches. Recognizing that unique circumstances, such as a search process, may arise due to various factors, including retirement or new callings for clergy, being part of the vestry during such times requires a shift in leadership dynamics. It presents an opportunity for prayer, discernment, and effective leadership.

A rector search process presents an extraordinary opportunity for the vestry to exercise leadership, wisdom, and discernment. It is crucial to remain focused on the church's mission and ministry while being flexible and welcoming to the new rector.

APPENDIX D: THE RECTOR'S EVALUATION
THE OUTLINE OF A BENEFICIAL PROCESS

O nce again, I refer you to the Diocese of Western Anglicans, whose list of resources is impressive. They have a specific process worked out and tested over time. I commend the document to you for your consideration. As with anything, your mileage may vary. That is, you will need to adapt it to your own circumstances.

Having said that, let me add my thoughts.

Evaluating the rector is crucial to ensure they meet the congregation's needs and effectively fulfill their role. However, finding the right person or process for evaluation can be challenging. Here are some recommendations for creating a successful evaluation process:

- Establish a formal, written evaluation plan: Develop a mutually agreed-upon program of reflection, discussion, and evaluation between the rector and the wardens. This plan should be revisited and improved annually, fostering a culture of continuous growth and learning.

- Recognize the importance of evaluating the rector: The rector should be aware of their performance from the congregation's perspective and their progress towards the parish's goals. Assessment helps ensure the congregation grows, the staff is well-trained, pastoral needs are met, and sermons are meaningful and biblically sound.
- Understand the unique nature of ministry: Evaluating a rector differs from evaluating other roles, as the ministry is about presence, prayer, and practices that engage the parish in the church's mission. Recognizing that ministry cannot be quantified solely by numbers or metrics is essential.
- Combine perspectives for a holistic evaluation: Since no single individual may be best suited to evaluate the rector, consider a combined approach. The rector can begin by self-assessing their role, focusing on aspects like parish culture, mission, preaching, prayer life, family life, and personal habits. This self-assessment can be shared with the wardens and the bishop.
- Engage in constructive dialogue with the bishop and wardens: Schedule a call with the bishop to review the self-assessment and seek advice, counsel, and prayer. Discuss the summarized self-assessment with the wardens, incorporating the bishop's insights.
- Involve the vestry for transparency and accountability: Share a redacted version of the self-assessment with the vestry, summarizing the process and outlining next steps for growth as a minister. This discussion creates accountability and allows for input from the broader leadership team.

BY FOLLOWING THESE BEST PRACTICES, THE EVALUATION process for the rector will be more effective and beneficial to both the rector and the congregation. Embracing a culture of continuous improvement and focusing on the unique aspects of ministry will help create a thriving parish that effectively serves its members and advances its mission.

APPENDIX E: AN ANGLICAN GLOSSARY

A COLLECTION OF TITLES, TERMS, AND TECHNICALS

Throughout this book, you might have encountered words that seemed familiar but foreign. These words looked like they belonged in a church and were easily pronounced in English, but you may have had trouble defining them.

Here, then, for your interest and information, is a partial glossary of terms and titles from the Anglican Church.

TITLES

The Rev. (The Reverend): A title used to address or refer to ordained clergy, such as priests or ministers, in both spoken and written communication.

The Very Rev. (The Very Reverend): A title used for the deans of cathedrals or other high-ranking clergy, signifying their seniority within the church hierarchy.

Archbishop: The highest-ranking bishop in a province, responsible for overseeing the work of other bishops and representing the province in the worldwide Anglican Communion. The title is often preceded by "The Most Rev." or "The Most Reverend."

Most Rev. (The Most Reverend): A title used to address or refer to archbishops in both spoken and written communication, indicating their seniority within the church hierarchy.

The Right Rev. (The Right Reverend): A title used to address or refer to bishops in both spoken and written communication, signifying their status within the church hierarchy.

Canon: A title given to some clergy members who have a specific role within the administration of a diocese or cathedral, such as serving on the bishop's staff or as a residentiary canon of a cathedral.

The Ven. (The Venerable): A title used for archdeacons, signifying their seniority and role in the administration of a diocese.

TERMS:

Anglicanism: The tradition of Christianity that developed from the Church of England, characterized by a distinctive theology, liturgy, and church structure.

Archbishop: The highest-ranking bishop in a province, responsible for overseeing the work of other bishops and representing the province in the worldwide Anglican Communion.

Book of Common Prayer (BCP): The foundational prayer book and liturgical guide for Anglican worship, containing the texts for the sacraments, prayers, and other services. Although any edition of the BCP in print is acceptable for use in the Anglican Church in North America, the standard BCP is the 2019 edition.

Bishop: An ordained minister who oversees a diocese's spiritual and administrative affairs, providing guidance and leadership to the priests and congregations within their jurisdiction.

Canon: A rule or guideline governing the beliefs, practices, and governance of the Anglican Church. Canons are developed and adopted by national, provincial, or diocesan governing bodies.

Chancel: The area of a church building near the altar, typically reserved for the clergy and choir during worship services.

Confirmation: A rite in which baptized Christians affirm their faith and commitment to Christ, often involving the laying on of hands by a bishop.

Diocese: A geographical region containing several churches and congregations, overseen by a bishop. In some cases, dioceses in the ACNA are formed non-geographically for theological or missional emphasis.

Eucharist: Also known as Holy Communion or the Lord's Supper, a sacrament in which bread and wine are consecrated and shared as a means of grace and a symbol of Christ's presence.

Evensong: A traditional Anglican evening worship service combining Evening Prayer and choral music elements.

Holy Orders: The sacrament of ordination in which individuals are set apart for ordained ministry as deacons, priests, or bishops.

Laity: Church members who are not ordained clergy, often involved in various roles and ministries within the church.

Liturgy: The structured form of worship used in Anglican services, including prayers, readings, hymns, and rituals.

Nave: The central area of a church building where the congregation sits during worship services.

Ordination: The process and ceremony by which individuals are set apart for ordained ministry as deacons, priests, or bishops.

Parish: A local congregation or community of Christians within a diocese, which a priest or other ordained minister leads.

Priest: An ordained minister responsible for leading worship, administering sacraments, and providing pastoral care to a congregation.

Rector: The priest in charge of a self-governing parish, responsible for its spiritual and administrative leadership.

Sacrament: A visible and outward sign of God's grace, instituted by Christ, which imparts spiritual benefits to believers. Anglicans recognize two primary sacraments: Baptism and the Eucharist.

Vestry: A group of laypeople elected or appointed to assist in the governance and administration of a parish, typically responsible for managing finances, property, and other practical matters.

TECHNICALS

Book of Common Prayer: The primary liturgical book containing the prayers, services, and rites used in the Anglican Church.

Chalice: The cup used to hold the wine during the Eucharist, symbolizing the blood of Christ.

Chancel: The area of the church containing the altar and choir, often separated from the nave by a screen or railing.

Ciborium: A covered container used to hold the consecrated bread (hosts) for distribution during Holy Communion.

Collect: A short prayer that "collects" the themes of the Scripture readings and liturgy, often recited by the priest during worship services.

Evensong: A traditional Anglican evening prayer service that includes choral music, Scripture readings, and prayers.

Lectern: A stand from which the Scripture readings and prayers are read during worship services.

Lectionary: A schedule of Scripture readings used in worship services, often following a three-year cycle.

Liturgical Colors: The colors of vestments and altar hangings that change according to the seasons of the church year (e.g., green for Ordinary Time, purple for Advent and Lent, white for Christmas and Easter).

Morning Prayer: A traditional Anglican morning prayer service, often including Scripture readings, prayers, and canticles, but not the Eucharist.

Narthex: The entrance area or vestibule of the church, often used for gathering and fellowship before or after services.

Nave: The main body of the church where the congregation sits during worship services.

Paschal Candle: A large, decorated candle lit during the Easter Vigil and other special services, symbolizing the light of Christ.

Paten: The plate used to hold the bread during the Eucharist, symbolizing the body of Christ.

Pulpit: A raised platform from which the preacher delivers the sermon during worship services.

Sacristy: A room where vestments, altar linens, and other liturgical items are stored and prepared for worship services.

Sanctuary: The sacred space within the church, often referring to the area around the altar.

Transept: The area of the church that extends perpendicular to the nave, creating a cross shape in the floor plan.

Vestments: The special garments worn by clergy and other ministers during worship services, symbolizing their roles and functions.

APPENDIX F: BISHOPS: FOR THE BENEFIT OR THE ESSENCE OF THE CHURCH
NICE TO HAVE? OR NEED TO HAVE?

Within Anglicanism, there has long been discussion about whether having bishops is "essential" (esse) or just "beneficial" (bene-esse) for the church. Is having bishops something essential to the life and structure of the church? Or is it merely a convenient tradition that could be changed? Anglicans have wrestled back and forth with this over the centuries. Let's delve into some of the key points around bishops being either indispensable or optional.

THE CASE FOR BISHOPS AS ESSENTIAL

Those who argue that having bishops is utterly essential point to several key reasons why Anglican churches cannot thrive without the episcopate as a distinct office of oversight.

HISTORICAL LINEAGE:

Bishops have existed in the church since New Testament times, originating with the appointing of apostolic successors like Matthias and James to lead local believers. This provides an unbroken lineage of authority and teaching passed down generationally. Abandoning bishops breaks continuity with 2,000 years of tradition.

SCRIPTURAL IMPLICATIONS

Verses like 1 Timothy 3, Titus 1, Acts 20, and 1 Peter 2 seem to imply an established office of bishop or overseer in the early church. Defenders argue that while not absolutely commanded, the biblical hints at least sanction the role of bishops we have received.

APOSTOLIC SUCCESSION

Anglican theology has long emphasized the passing down of authority from the apostles through each generation's bishops. This "tactile" succession ensures valid ordinations and sacraments. Eliminating bishops could compromise this.

ORDER AND GOVERNANCE

Bishops provide unified leadership, doctrine, and discipline across regional churches. This maintains proper order and helps prevent fragmentation, instability, and confusion. The Anglican ethos has favored order.

Those advocating for the essential nature of bishops urge maintaining this historic office to stay rooted in tradition, preserve apostolic succession, uphold governance and order, and follow Scriptural guidance - even if done flexibly.

THE CASE FOR BISHOPS AS BENEFICIAL ONLY

On the other hand, some Anglicans have argued that while the office of bishop may be useful, helpful, or even advisable, it is not strictly mandatory. Here are some key points they make:

BIBLICAL AMBIGUITY

Nowhere does the New Testament command one fixed form of church government. The earliest churches seemed to handle leadership in various ways. God can bless polities like Presbyterianism that don't include bishops.

TERMINOLOGY

"Bishop" and "presbyter/elder" were sometimes interchangeable terms in the New Testament, hinting at possible fluidity between the roles early on. The sharp distinction came later.

ADAPTABILITY

Even defenders of bishops have made provisions for non-episcopal ordinations when deemed valid, as with Methodist ministries. Strict succession is not always required.

PRIESTHOOD OF BELIEVERS

While order has value, authority in the church resides with the whole people of God, not just bishops. The wider spirit-led body must have a voice along with overseers.

POTENTIAL ABUSES

Hierarchical authority under imperfect bishops has often led to corruption, coercion, and abuses of power. Checks and balances should temper episcopal power.

ESSENTIALS

Faithful biblical teaching, preaching, and sacraments can continue without bishops, guided by godly discipline. Apostolic succession is valuable but not the heart of the gospel.

In this view, episcopal governance is seen as a changeable human tradition that can be adapted as needed, not a divine mandate. The essence of the church remains with or without formal bishops.

NAVIGATING THE DISCUSSION

This ancient debate continues in modern Anglican circles: to what degree are bishops indispensable or optional comes down to differing views on church history, theology, and practical governance? There are thoughtful cases on both sides.

Perhaps a balanced Anglican approach is to appreciate the wisdom of the episcopate inherited from history while also recognizing that bishops are not the ultimate foundation of Christ's Church, which rests on Him alone. Bishops serve a vital purpose for unity and order but must be held accountable.

As we engage in this sensitive discussion, may we do so with humble spirits, respecting those of differing views, for the sake of our shared Anglican witness to the timeless gospel of Jesus Christ.

APPENDIX G: WHAT ABOUT THE VESTRY WARDENS?

A STORY OF THANKSGIVING

My last summer at Christ Church in Plano, Texas, where I served, was a time of saying goodbye to many amazing friends and co-laborers from the past 31 years of ministry. I am sure you can imagine how emotional and wonderful it was to spend time over coffee, dinners, conversations, and after-church events thanking people for their love and support.

My resignation as Rector was a surprise to most people, including me. I had imagined staying in that role for another ten years. I honestly had thought that. But when I turned 60, I had a profound impression from God that I was to step aside and let a younger leader be called. I was sad to leave this great church, but I was confident that the Lord had given me this clear direction.

There was one last dinner I wanted to host. I intended to honor and thank all the senior wardens who had served at Christ Church. I made a list of everyone who had served in that capacity and invited them to my home for supper. Unlike the meetings they had attended in their tenure as senior warden, there would be no minutes, no formal reports, no financial reviews, and no votes cast. I only had one item on the agenda: thanksgiving.

Thirty-two men and women had stood with me for over three decades of work and ministry at Christ Church. One of the former wardens, Matt, had died a few years previously. One had moved away. Another warden and I had had a falling out, and he graciously chose not to attend. One of the wardens from the past had joined a Roman Catholic church and, after his wife died, had become a Roman Catholic priest. One had joined another denomination. But that night, 27 wardens came to my home for my last vestry meeting, as unofficial as it was.

REMEMBERING GOD'S FAITHFULNESS

I had nothing but thanks to express to these friends, and they were all friends. They had been part of a story of growth and challenge during my time at Christ Church. We all shared memories of some hard-won accomplishments and some deeply felt losses. I had prepared only one question for the group that gathered in my living room after dinner.

Emotion caught in my throat as I called the meeting to order. I thanked them all for coming. I expressed what it had meant to me to lead this church for so many years. And then I asked them the question I had prepared: "What do you remember of God's faithfulness in your time as a Senior Warden?"

The stories began. Some early wardens remembered the financial thin ice we used to skate on every year, waiting for December (and the Lord) to make us whole. A few recounted when we "sent off" one of our many new church plants to a nearby community. Some told stories of personal growth as they learned to pray through some of the large vision-correction moments we faced. They all had prayed with me through the many years we wrestled with our denominational struggles in the Episcopal Church. Most everyone in the room remembered a building project. In fact, if you were a senior warden at Christ Church, chances were very good that you had been part of one of our seven back-to-back 3-year capital campaigns to either build a building or pay off a debt.

If we had had the entire evening, we would have remembered the land purchases we negotiated, the architects and builders we interviewed and hired, and the policies we had to enact as we expanded our campus. We may also have remembered the architect we fired, the personnel issues we struggled with, the search processes we endured, the missionaries and bishops we hosted, the field trips we took, and endless coffees we drank over the plans we made, prayers we prayed, and fears we shared.

My leadership of our Vestry during those three decades was not without trials and hardships. But they were glad to be there. And I was glad that every one of them had come.

THE WARDEN AS WINGMAN

The wardens were my wingmen, one by one, year by year. They were the ones that I knew I could call when I shouldn't call anyone else. Each warden had my back. If we disagreed in private meetings, we always agreed in public. A few times, my wardens "covered" for me when I made errors in judgment.

I remember once when I had to terminate a youth worker. It got ugly. The parents demanded a meeting. They wanted to know why. There was sufficient cause for the termination of this youth leader, but I did not want to disclose any details. I did not want to trigger a lawsuit. I just stood before the group of parents and hurt teenagers and asked them to trust my judgment. There was some murmuring and vocalizing, but I stood my ground.

Before it worsened, the senior warden stood up, walked to the front of the room, and joined me at my side. He took the microphone and spoke to the room. He said he knew the situation and that I had made the right decision. The murmuring ended, and the meeting dispersed. He had my back.

In the early days of my ministry, a wise priest told me never to talk to the vestry about my salary or any aspect of my personal compensation. I never did. Not once. But the wardens did. Most every year in the fall, they would come to me and ask how I was doing financially. I would be frank with them. If it was tight for us, I would tell them. If we were doing okay, I would tell them. As the budget was presented at one of the last meetings of every year, the wardens would ask me to leave the meeting room and go home. They would talk about my compensation and determine what increase, if any, I would receive.

The tradition in the Episcopal Church (where I came from) was to have two wardens, junior and senior. In some churches, the rector selects the senior warden, and the vestry selects the junior warden. Sometimes, this is a matter of tradition and/or by-law.

I worked in a slightly different situation. I appointed the senior warden and asked the vestry to elect a junior warden. I met with them monthly to review and prepare for vestry meetings and discuss other issues and challenges. When the senior warden would rotate off the vestry, I would appoint the junior warden to that role, and the vestry would elect another. In this way, the vestry would have some hand in selecting the senior warden by electing the junior warden. I will admit that I routinely nominated a person to serve as junior warden, knowing he would soon be senior warden.

All of my senior wardens had been junior wardens before.

The wardens and I formed a three-person partnership year by year. We were an executive committee. They were my lay partners; they helped me see the world of the church through the eyes of people in the pews. And every one of my senior wardens had been the junior warden the year before.

ROLE AND DUTIES OF WARDENS

We can all agree that "warden" is an odd name. The church is not a prison, and the rector is not an inmate! But the term dates from the 14th century when a non-clerical (lay) person was appointed in every parish in England as the intermediary between the rector and the parish. The term is unique to the Anglican polity.

The canons of the church do not tightly prescribe the role of the warden. Most congregations and rector develop their ideas about the role in a particular congregation. The role will probably ebb and flow to fit the personality of the congregation, the personality of the warden, the rector, and the size of the church. The role of the warden is not an honorary title. It is a working title. It is a serious and vital role on the vestry.

How serious? If the rector's position is, for any reason, vacated or absented, the senior warden is the one who will lead the church. The interim role does not default to an assisting priest or the older staff member automatically. No one is ever "promoted" in Anglican polity. Instead, the senior warden is put in charge of the congregation. They are responsible for keeping the church doors open for public worship, appointing or leading a search process to find, elect, and call a new rector, and maintaining the financial obligations of the parish.

If you are reading this and you are a senior warden or considering becoming the next one, you probably had a catch in your breath with this last paragraph. Your heart may have skipped a beat. You thought to yourself that, in the event of the rector's departure, you would be in charge of the congregation. But you can relax. In normal circumstances, the bishop is involved immediately and will help define a plan forward, including appointing an Interim Rector to assume the priestly functions of the rector. So, relax, friend. You must become the leader of the vestry, but you don't have to preach a sermon!

THREE QUESTIONS EVERY SENIOR WARDEN SHOULD ASK

As we will see, the senior warden has significant responsibility and influence. Choosing who will serve as senior warden is usually left to the rector, and it should be remembered that the role is not honorary. A newly recruited senior warden might feel flattered or honored to be asked to serve the church in this way. That is a good initial response, but I advise each candidate or senior warden nominee to prayerfully and thoughtfully answer these three questions in succession.

- Do I believe in the stated and directional mission of this congregation?
- Do I believe in the call and character of the Rector to lead this congregation?
- Would I want to go on vacation or 'hang out' with this Rector?

The first two questions concern the clarity of the vision and the leader's character, but the third question concerns chemistry. Is there a friendship and appreciation for this person (Rector) such that I would want to spend time and invest in an ongoing relationship?

APPENDIX H: CANONS EVERY VESTRY SHOULD KNOW

ANGLICAN POLITY AND GOVERNANCE DETAILS

T he Constitution and Canons of the Anglican Church in North America have clear directions for the primacy of the local congregation and vestries. According to the Constitution and Canons of the ACNA, these are the most pertinent items ratified by the Inaugural Provincial Assembly in June 2009 and amended by the fifth Provincial Assembly in June 2019.

FROM THE CONSTITUTION:

ARTICLE III: THE MISSION OF THE PROVINCE

The mission of the Province is to extend the Kingdom of God by so presenting Jesus Christ in the power of the Holy Spirit that people everywhere will come to put their trust in God through Him, know Him as Savior and serve Him as Lord in the fellowship of the Church. The chief agents of this mission to extend the Kingdom of God are the people of God.

ARTICLE IV: THE STRUCTURE OF THE PROVINCE

The fundamental agency of mission in the Province is the local congregation.

ARTICLE XII: OWNERSHIP OF PROPERTY

All church property, both real and personal, owned by each member congregation now and in the future is and shall be solely and exclusively owned by each member congregation and shall not be subject to any trust interest in favor of the Province or any other claim of ownership arising out of the canon law of this Province. Where property is held in a different manner by any diocese or grouping, such ownership shall be preserved.

FROM THE CANONS:

TITLE I: CANON 6 – OF CONGREGATIONS

Section 1 – Concerning Congregational Mission

The fundamental agency of the mission of the Church to extend the Kingdom of God is the local congregation. The chief agents of this mission are the people of God.

SECTION 2 – CONCERNING CONGREGATIONS

A congregation in this Church is a gathered group of Christians who have organized and function in accordance with the canons of this Church attached to a diocese and under the oversight of a Bishop. Every congregation of the Church belongs to the Church by union with a Diocese of the Church or through a Diocese-in-Formation. A congregation of this Church is a gathering where the pure Word of God is preached and the sacraments are duly administered according to Christ's ordinance (Article XIX).

Section 3 – Concerning Organization

Every congregation shall be established in accordance with the laws of the State or jurisdiction where situated, shall handle its own finances, and shall carry insurance coverage in amounts specified by its Diocese, except in those Dioceses with constitutional or canonical provisions to the contrary.

Section 4 – Concerning Congregational Clergy and Lay Employees

1. No Rector may be called to or dismissed from a congregation without the consent of the Bishop. No other clergy may be called or dismissed from a congregation without consultation with the Bishop. A diocese may adopt canons not in conflict with this section.

2. All assistant clergy and lay employees of the congregation shall serve under the direction of and at the pleasure of the Rector except as may be otherwise provided under local law.

Section 5 – Concerning Governing Boards

There shall be a governing board of each congregation, often known as the vestry, which is chosen and serves according to applicable laws, diocesan canons, and the congregational by-laws. The Presbyter in charge of the congregation shall always be a member of the governing board and its presiding officer except as provided by diocesan canon. The governing board is responsible for the temporalities of the congregation and, except where otherwise provided by canon, supports the clergy in the spiritual leadership of the congregation.

Section 6 – Concerning Property Ownership

All congregational property, real and personal, owned by a member congregation is and shall be solely and exclusively owned by the congregation and shall not be subject to any trust in favor of the Province or other claim of ownership arising out of the canon law of the Church; neither may any Diocese assert any such claim over the property of any of its congregations without the express written consent of the congregation. Where property is held in a different manner by any Diocese or grouping, such ownership shall be preserved.

Canon 9 – Of Finances Section 1 – Concerning the Tithe

The biblical tithe is the minimum standard of giving to support the Mission of the Church and should be taught and encouraged at every level in the Church.

Canon 10 – Of the Laity Section 3 – Concerning Membership in the Church

Membership in the Church requires that a person has received the Sacrament of Baptism with water in the Name of the Father, and of the Son, and of the Holy Spirit, and that such a person be accepted as a member of the Church by a congregation of this Church in compliance with the Constitution of the Church. Such a person is a baptized member of the Church. A confirmed member is a baptized member who has been confirmed or received by a Bishop of the Church. Dioceses and congregations may establish the norm and standards for membership in good standing.

Title III: Canon 7 – Of Rectors and Other Congregation Clergy

Norms for the calling, duties, and support of Rectors and other Clergy, and the dissolution of a pastoral relation shall be provided by each Diocese. Rectors shall be domiciled in the diocese to which their congregation belongs.

THOUGH IT MAY SEEM OUTDATED, MEMBERSHIP IS essential for electing vestry members who, alongside the Rector, guide the church's growth and mission. By redefining membership to include mission and engagement, congregations can foster a more active and engaged community.

APPENDIX I: VESTRY IN-SERVICE AND TRAINING

IDEAS AND OUTLINES FOR TRAINING AND TEACHING

The rector should work with the vestry to assess the culture around them and how their church is reaching people in their community. Or not. The vestry must be challenged to think critically and assess how their church impacts the world around them. The rector is tasked with activating this elected group of members of the congregation. He should find ways to bring the congregation's ministry into focus and ask critical questions such as, "What are we doing, and why are we doing it?" This should be done at least annually. Anything less than a robust effort to address this question is an abdication of the duties of the office of the rector.

It is important to remember that there is only one rector, and only he can ask these critical questions. The vestry must be empowered to take an active role in the church's ministry and to work towards fulfilling the church's mission in the world. It is the rector's responsibility to lead the vestry towards a deeper understanding of its role in the church and to ensure that its programs align with its mission.

This book has a few chapters that could be used to teach, train, or develop vestry members. Some chapters could be subjects for a staff in-service or a vestry retreat. To facilitate those moments, I have developed some discussion questions based on the content of a few of these chapters.

FROM CHAPTER ONE: YOUR CHURCH CHANGES THE WORLD

- **Your Amazing Church:** How can we, as a vestry, better understand and internalize the importance of the church's timeless mission and its role in the broader global community? How can we ensure that our church remains focused on this mission, transcending time and culture, as it has for the past 2000 years?
- **The Great Commission and the Church:** In light of the Great Commission being given to a gathered group, how can we foster a sense of unity and shared responsibility within our congregation? How can we encourage each member to actively participate in the church's mission, individually and collectively?
- **The Church Resilient:** Like the example of EDS, many organizations fail because they cannot adapt to changing circumstances. As a vestry, how can we proactively anticipate changes and challenges that may affect our church and its mission? How can we cultivate a mindset of adaptability and resilience in the face of these challenges?
- **Stewardship and Leadership:** As church leaders, we are called to be faithful stewards of this world-changing organization. How can we hold ourselves accountable in our roles, prioritizing the church's mission above administrative tasks and program-building? How can we

develop and maintain a strong, Christ-centered, Holy Spirit-empowered leadership team?

- **Renewal and Reformation:** The church has a history of self-renewal and reformation in response to various challenges. How can our vestry promote a culture of reflection, growth, and renewal within our congregation? How can we be open to the transformative work of the Holy Spirit in our church and its mission?

FROM CHAPTER FOUR: BIG CHURCH, SMALL CHURCH

- What type of "school typology" would you classify our congregation as - Home School, Grade School, High School, or College Church? How do our size and culture contribute to this classification?
- How does our congregation's size impact the vestry's role, and what unique challenges do we face in terms of leadership and growth?
- How can we leverage the strengths of our current congregation size to grow and reach more people in our community? What specific strategies can we implement to achieve this goal?
- In what ways can we improve communication and coordination among our leadership team, both within the vestry and with our rector and other clergy members? What structures or processes can we implement to ensure effective collaboration and decision-making?

FROM CHAPTER FIVE: INSIDE THE MISSION-DRIVEN CHURCH

Consider taking 30 minutes at each of the next six vestry meetings and address some of the issues raised in the chapter on organizing for the church's mission. Don't start with a blank slate, though. The rector should prepare ahead of time a full list of programs and ministries that address each of the six areas of adult ministry.

- What are the elements of our worship ministry (our system)? Are our people trained to work together to make worship the high moment every week?
- Are we teaching children and playing with adults or vice-versa?
- Do our teaching programs include serious training for growing disciples of Christ?
- How are we carrying out the dictum of Archbishop William Temple? Are our outreach and social ministry evangelistic?
- How organized and redundant are our communication channels? Do we work in step together on our messaging, or is everyone randomly trying to get the word out?
- Does our vestry understand its role in this area? Are its members over-involved in the programming of our parish?
- Why do you think people join your congregation? Why do they stay in your church?
- How many groups or cliques are there in the congregation? Is there enough for anyone wanting to be in one to be welcomed?

TEN QUESTIONS TO GROW ON

Most churches want to grow. Or shall I tip my hand and admit that, in my opinion, most churches should want to grow? A growing church is a church that is constantly refreshing itself with new leaders, new programs, new emphasis, and renewed passion for the Great Commission.

However, most churches struggle to grow. Irrespective of current size, many churches reach a 'steady state' where the people who attend the church are very happy going; those who used to attend are happy not going; and those who have never attended the church are ignorant of what they are missing. But this is a sad state, in my opinion. The church of the New Testament grew. It was a sign of the Holy Spirit's movement and the Gospel's compelling message. The community around the church—Jerusalem—needed the church to grow. And the Great Commission mandate given by Jesus himself required the church to grow.

But still, in our own day, how can we help the church to capture its growth potential?

Here are ten questions clergy, staff, and vestry should consider asking, discussing, and processing as a leadership team. Some vestries and staff may want to spend the time and money to hire a consultant to help them address these questions, determine their answers and responses, and then map out a plan to put answers into action.

1. How can we continually evaluate and enhance our worship experience to ensure it is engaging, relevant, and spiritually nourishing for both current and potential new members? Are there opportunities to explore different worship styles, music, or liturgical elements that can appeal to a diverse range of individuals?

2. How can we encourage active participation and engagement from our congregation during worship services? Are there ways to involve members in planning and executing worship services, such as inviting them to share their talents, testimonies, or insights, to foster a sense of ownership and belonging among the congregation?

3. How can we utilize our Evangelistic Outreach and Discipleship Training systems more effectively to attract new members and foster spiritual growth within our existing congregation? Are there specific outreach programs or discipleship initiatives we can develop to address the needs of our surrounding community?

4. How can we create a welcoming and inclusive environment for newcomers, making it easy for them to connect with existing members and get involved in church activities? Are there any barriers or challenges we must address to improve the experience for new members?

5. In what ways can we leverage our Redundant Communication system to not only inform our current congregation but also engage and attract potential new members? How can we utilize social media and other digital platforms to reach a wider audience and share our church's message and mission?

6. How can we identify and support the development of lay leaders within our congregation who can help drive the growth of our church and its ministries? Are there opportunities to provide leadership training and mentoring for those interested in taking on more responsibility?

7. How can we improve our Administration system to ensure that our church operates efficiently and professionally, instilling confidence in both current and

prospective members that our church is well-managed and trustworthy?

8. How can we regularly evaluate and adapt our Pastoral Connections system to ensure that it continues to meet the needs of a growing congregation? Are there opportunities to expand or diversify our pastoral care offerings to support the diverse needs of our members better?

9. Are there any partnerships or collaborations with other community organizations, businesses, or institutions that we can explore to help raise our church's profile and engage with a broader audience?

10. How can we effectively measure our congregation's growth and identify areas for improvement or areas where we are experiencing success? What key performance indicators or metrics can we use to track our progress and guide our growth strategy?

ACKNOWLEDGMENTS FOR THE SECOND EDITION

This book began as *The Rector and the Vestry*, published in 2020 after a young church planter shared his need for guidance on Anglican polity. His vestry's lack of experience with our traditions inspired the first edition. Similarly, a conversation about a perplexed vestry's minimal understanding of the bishop's role seeded this new, expanded version.

Thus, *The Rector, the Vestry, and the Bishop* was born to provide a more robust resource for leaders navigating our denomination's governance.

In the life cycle of a book, many deserve thanks for bringing the first edition to fruition. But a second edition multiplies the gratitude further. The number of people to acknowledge is abundant; too many to name here. Still, some must be mentioned.

I am thankful for the rectors I coach, whose passion for ministry inspires me daily. Their commitment to leading well makes my work a joy. Sincere thanks to the donors whose generosity affords me time for writing; this book would not exist without you.

Most of all, I am overwhelmed with gratitude for the decades of ministry I've been granted. It has been the privilege of a lifetime to serve our Lord in His church. The lessons learned span more years than I can count.

My wife has been a constant source of love, support, and encouragement through it all. I could not ask for a better partner in life and ministry. Her patience and affirmation mean the world, as always.

To the many unnamed who have shaped this book: you have my deepest appreciation. I hope and pray that these pages may equip leaders at every level of our beloved Anglican Church to serve with vision, wisdom, and love.

To God be the glory.

David Roseberry

BIBLIOGRAPHY

WEBSITES

AnglicanCompass.com
Leaderworks.org
AnglicanChurch.net
Churchlawandtax.com
WesternAnglicans.org

BOOKS

Giving Up by David Roseberry
A Field Guide for Giving by David Roseberry
Inspiring Generosity by David Roseberry
Canoeing the Mountains by Tod Bolsinger
The Coming Revolution in Church Economics by Mark DeYmaz
A Failure of Nerve by Edwin H. Friedman
Our Character at Work by Todd D. Hunter
Death by Meeting by Patrick Lencioni
The Trellis and the Vine: The Ministry Mind-Shift That Changes Everything by
    Colin Marshall and Tony Payne
Beyond Business as Usual: Vestry Leadership Development by Neal O. Michell
A Spirituality of Fundraising by Henri J. M. Nouwen
Robert's Rules of Order
Finance for Non-financial Managers by Gene Siciliano
Next: Pastoral Succession That Works by William Vanderbloemen and Warren Bird
Search: The Pastoral Search Committee Handbook by William Vanderbloemen
The Vestry Handbook by Christopher L. Webber

ABOUT THE AUTHOR

 David Roseberry has been an ordained Anglican minister for over 40 years. He was the founding Rector of Christ Church in Plano, Texas, for over 30 years. Currently, he is the Executive Director of the non-profit ministry of LeaderWorks, which serves congregations and leaders in the Anglican Church in North America. He is a preacher, bible teacher, and speaker with a growing ministry through his numerous books. Check out his Amazon Author page.

He also leads life-changing pilgrimages to Israel and other historic places of the Christian faith. Join us! Information is available at the LeaderWorks website, www.leaderworks.org.

He and his wife, Fran, live in Plano, Texas. They have five children and five grandchildren.

Stay in touch with the ministry of LeaderWorks.

ALSO BY DAVID H. ROSEBERRY

DEEPEN YOUR SPIRITUAL LIFE

The Last Will and Testament of the Apostle Paul

The Ordinary Ways of God: Inside the Book of Ruth

The Psalm on the Cross: A Journey to the Heart of Jesus through Psalm 22

When the Lord is My Shepherd: Finding Hope in a Hard Time

The Giving Life: Why it is More Blessed to Give than to Receive

The First 24: One Man. One Mission. One Day — Jesus of Nazareth

BOOKS ABOUT GENEROSITY

Giving Up: How Giving to God Renews Hearts, Changes Minds, and Empowers Ministry

A Field Guide for Giving: Increasing Generosity in the Local Church

Inspiring Generosity: The 10-Step Program for Highly Successful Annual Stewardship Campaigns

---

Authors who publish books independently rely on readers to offer honest reviews on platforms like Amazon or Goodreads. Please take the time to tell others about this book or any of the others you have read. Your comments are deeply appreciated.

If you have questions or suggestions about this book or any others, please contact me at David@LeaderWorks.org. All of these titles are available at bulk rate discounts by contacting me.

Made in the USA
Monee, IL
13 January 2025

76777216R00118